STRIPPED BUT NOT DEFEATED

PASTOR DR. CLAUDINE BENJAMIN

For more information or to book an event, contact: inspiredtowinsouls@gmail.com

Published by:

Editor: Cleveland O. McLeish (Author C. Orville McLeish)

ISBN: 978-1-965635-76-6 (paperback)

ABOUT THE AUTHOR

Pastor Claudine Benjamin is a passionate preacher, prophetic voice, and purpose-driven author who ministers with compassion, authenticity, and power. With a heart for the broken, the weary, and the overlooked, she boldly declares the truth that healing is possible, even after life has stripped you bare.

Having endured seasons of deep personal loss, hardship, and restoration, Pastor Claudine writes from a place of experience, empathy, and anointing. Her ministry is rooted in the belief that pain has a purpose, and what the enemy meant for evil, God will use for His glory.

As a voice of encouragement and empowerment, she equips others to rise from the ruins, reclaim their identity in Christ, and walk boldly into their calling. Through her books, sermons, and mentorship, she continues to help people around the world discover that they are not what they've been through—they are who God says they are.

Pastor Claudine is the author of multiple life-changing books focused on inner healing, purpose, restoration, and the power of the gospel. She is committed to reaching souls, rebuilding lives, and releasing hope.

Stripped but Not Defeated is her call to the crushed, the discarded, and the defeated—reminding them that the story is not over, and the best is still yet to come.

DEDICATION

This book is dedicated to every person who has walked through the fire, stood in the ashes, and questioned whether anything would ever rise from the rubble.

To the weary warrior who has been stripped of identity, relationships, purpose, or peace—this is for you. You may have lost much, but you did not lose God.

To those who have been dropped, forgotten, betrayed, or broken—I see you. God sees you. And He has not changed His mind about you.

I also dedicate this to the survivors, the rebuilders, the wounded worshippers, and the silent strugglers who kept pressing when quitting seemed easier.

And most of all, I dedicate this to the One who never left me in my stripped place—Jesus Christ, my Savior and Restorer, the One who clothed me again with righteousness and gave me a reason to stand.

ACKNOWLEDGMENT

First, I acknowledge my heavenly Father—Jehovah Rapha, my Healer. Thank You for not leaving me in the dust of my brokenness. Thank You for carrying me through the seasons where I felt exposed, empty, and undone. This book is the fruit of grace, and Your faithfulness is the ink behind every word.

To my family—thank you for walking with me through the seasons of stripping and believing in the oil that would still flow from me. Your love has been my anchor in deep waters.

To my ministry family and spiritual mentors—thank you for interceding, supporting, and reminding me that purpose is often birthed from pain.

To every reader who picks up this book, know this: your story matters. Your scars are not signs of shame, but signs of survival. I honor your journey, your fight, and your resilience. I pray this book becomes a mirror of healing and a mantle of strength you wear proudly.

Finally, to every silent warrior who's still in the process—this book was written with you in mind. You may be stripped now, but you will stand again.

TABLE OF CONTENTS

About the Author iii

Dedication v

Acknowledgment vii

Introduction: The Stripping Season—But Not the End 11

Part I

The Stripping Process

Chapter 1: When Everything Is Taken 17

Chapter 2: Naked Before God – The Place of Exposure 21

Chapter 3: Loss, Pain, and the Breaking of Pride 27

Chapter 4: When People Walk Away 33

Chapter 5: From Glory to Ground Zero 39

Part II

The Fight to Keep Going

Chapter 6: Holding On with Nothing Left 47

Chapter 7: The Battle in the Mind 53

Chapter 8: Silence, Shame, and Solitude 59

Chapter 9: Learning to Trust Again 65

Chapter 10: The Power of Tears and Transparency 71

Part III

Standing in the Middle of the Ruins

Chapter 11: Stripped but Still Breathing....79
Chapter 12: Worship in the Wilderness....85
Chapter 13: When Faith Is All You Have....91
Chapter 14: Rediscovering Identity Without the Extras....97
Chapter 15: The God Who Sees You Naked and Still Calls You...103

Part IV

The Unseen Victory

Chapter 16: What Was Not Taken From You....111
Chapter 17: Beauty in Brokenness....117
Chapter 18: Lessons Only Stripping Can Teach....123
Chapter 19: From Stripped to Strengthened....129
Chapter 20: The Re-Clothing—What God Puts on You After the Stripping....135
Chapter 21: You Are Not What Was Taken....143
Conclusion: From Stripped to Strengthened to Sent....149

INTRODUCTION

THE STRIPPING SEASON–BUT NOT THE END

There comes a moment in every believer's life when the wind of adversity blows so fiercely that it seems everything familiar is being ripped away. Identity, security, comfort, relationships, routines—all feel exposed, vulnerable, and undone. This is what I call the stripping season. It is the moment when what once covered us—titles, positions, people, approval, and even self-made strength—is pulled back so that only what God planted remains.

But hear this truth clearly: stripping is not the end. It is the beginning of divine clarity.

Stripping in the kingdom is never about shame or punishment—it's about preparation. Just as a tree loses its leaves in the fall, not to die, but to survive the winter and thrive in the spring, God permits the stripping to realign us with His greater purpose. Stripping eliminates what cannot sustain us for where He is taking us. It reveals what is essential, what is true, and what must be let go in order to walk in victory, healed and whole.

In the natural, when something is stripped—be it wood, land, or even dignity—it seems destroyed. But spiritually, God uses the stripping season to remove false identities, idols, distractions, and dependencies. He uses it to deepen trust, to uncover buried wounds, and to awaken the soul to something greater than survival: surrender and transformation.

You may feel like you've lost everything. You may be walking through the darkest valley of your life, stripped of answers, friends, finances, or even the will to keep moving. But God wants you to know: You are not defeated. You are being redefined.

This book is a journey for every person who has ever walked through a stripping season. It is for those who have cried themselves to sleep, wondered if God still saw them, and questioned if anything beautiful could come from the ashes of their life. It is for those who have been misunderstood, mishandled, and mistaken for weak when, in fact, they were in the middle of divine surgery.

As we journey through the pages ahead, you will encounter biblical characters who were stripped but not destroyed—Joseph, stripped of his coat but not his dream; Job, stripped of possessions but not his faith; Naomi, stripped of family but not her purpose; Jesus, stripped on the cross but victorious in resurrection.

You will also find encouragement, healing, and hope for your own season of stripping. This is not your ending. It is your turning point. God is removing what cannot go with you so He can replace it with what was always meant for you.

So don't despise the stripping. Embrace it. There is oil in the crushing, beauty in the brokenness, and purpose in the pain. And when it is all said and done, you will emerge not just restored, but rebuilt stronger than ever.

This is your reminder: You are stripped, but not defeated.

PART I

THE STRIPPING PROCESS

CHAPTER I

WHEN EVERYTHING IS TAKEN

There comes a point in life where the stripping feels merciless. Everything that once gave you comfort, identity, or security is suddenly gone. Your finances may crumble, your relationships fall apart, your health declines, or your dreams are dashed in a single moment. It is in this place that we meet the first character in our journey—Job, the man who was stripped of everything yet remained undefeated in his faith.

Character Focus: Job – The Stripped but Unshaken Servant

Job was a man of great wealth, honor, and righteousness. The Bible describes him as **"blameless and upright; he feared God and shunned evil" (Job 1:1, NIV).** He was not just blessed materially—he was blessed spiritually. He had a large family, numerous possessions, and a respected name in his community.

But in a sudden and violent turn of events, Job lost it all. His livestock was stolen or destroyed, his servants were murdered, and worst of all, his children died in a tragic accident. If that wasn't enough, he was afflicted with painful sores from head to toe. In the eyes of the world, Job was stripped of everything.

Yet what we must note is how Job responded:

> **"Naked I came from my mother's womb, and naked I will depart. The Lord gave and the Lord has taken away; may the name of the Lord be praised." — Job 1:21 (NIV)**

Job teaches us that being stripped does not mean being separated from God. In fact, sometimes, the stripping is what proves our faith is real. It is in the fire that the purity of gold is revealed. Job did not curse God, though everything around him and everyone near him—including his wife—told him to do so (**see Job 2:9-10**).

Instead, Job chose worship. He chose faith. He chose to acknowledge the sovereignty of God, even in his suffering.

The Spiritual Significance of Being Stripped

In our modern context, being stripped might not look like the loss of cattle or ancient riches. It could be the closing of a business you built from the ground up. It might be a betrayal that cuts to your core. It might be the diagnosis you didn't see coming or the silent nights where your prayers feel unanswered.

Yet the stripping reveals what's beneath the surface. The question becomes: When all is taken, what remains?

> **"But he knows the way that I take; when he has tested me, I will come forth as gold." — Job 23:10 (NIV)**

God is not trying to destroy you in your stripping season. He is purifying you, refining your heart, and separating your faith from your flesh. It hurts—but it is holy.

Reflection from the Cross: Jesus Was Stripped Too

Even Jesus, our Lord and Savior, was stripped before His crucifixion. The Roman soldiers removed His garments, mocked Him, and left Him exposed (**see Matthew 27:28**). He was humiliated and left vulnerable before men—but His purpose remained untouched.

You are not defeated because you've been stripped. Jesus was too—and He rose in power.

Scriptures for Meditation

- Job 1:20–22
- Job 23:10
- 2 Corinthians 4:8–10
- Romans 8:35–39
- Matthew 27:28
- Isaiah 61:3

CHAPTER 2

NAKED BEFORE GOD – THE PLACE OF EXPOSURE

There is a moment in every believer's journey where everything familiar fades away. The outer layers we used to protect ourselves—titles, positions, status, possessions—are peeled back. Suddenly, we are naked before God. There is nothing left to hide behind, no mask to wear, and no reputation to uphold. All that remains is the real you, exposed and vulnerable.

This is not a punishment. This is holy exposure. And no one represents this place better than Adam and Eve, the first to experience the painful revelation of nakedness before a holy God.

Character Focus: Adam and Eve – From Covered to Confronted

In the Garden of Eden, Adam and Eve lived in perfect union with God. There was no shame in their nakedness. Genesis 2:25 tells us,

> **"Adam and his wife were both naked, and they felt no shame." (NIV).**

They were fully known, fully loved, and fully accepted. There was no fear in their transparency because sin had not yet entered the world. They walked openly before God—spiritually and physically uncovered.

But when they disobeyed God by eating from the tree of the knowledge of good and evil, their eyes were opened, and for the first time, they felt shame. They were still in the same garden, with the same God, but now they were afraid of being seen.

> **"Then the eyes of both of them were opened, and they realized they were naked; so they sewed fig leaves together and made coverings for themselves." — Genesis 3:7 (NIV)**

God came walking in the garden, as He had done before, but Adam and Eve hid (**see Genesis 3:8**). Not only were they stripped by sin—they were now spiritually separated from the One who had made them.

The Power of Exposure

When God asked, **"Where are you?"** in Genesis 3:9, it wasn't because He didn't know their location. It was a divine question meant to reveal their condition. Adam replied:

> **"I heard you in the garden, and I was afraid because I was naked; so I hid." — Genesis 3:10 (NIV)**

This is what happens when we are stripped: fear, shame, and hiding often follow. But God doesn't ask where you are to condemn you—He asks to restore you.

The exposure was never meant to humiliate Adam and Eve, and it's not meant to humiliate you either. It's an invitation to return to the presence of God without pretense, without masks, and without trying to cover what only He can clothe in grace.

God Will Cover What He Confronts

Even after pronouncing consequences for their sin, God did something incredible. He covered them.

> **"The Lord God made garments of skin for Adam and his wife and clothed them." — Genesis 3:21 (NIV)**

The fig leaves they made were temporary and insufficient, much like our own efforts to cover our weaknesses, failures, or shame. But God's covering was sacrificial—blood had to be shed to clothe them. This was a foreshadowing of Christ, whose blood would one day be shed to cover all mankind.

You may be in a season where you feel spiritually or emotionally naked. You feel seen, but not in a comforting way—in a painful, shameful way. But God does not expose what He won't heal. He does not uncover you to destroy you—He uncovers you to redeem you.

Lessons from the Place of Exposure

1. **Exposure reveals the truth, not to shame but to sanctify.**

God doesn't want your filters—He wants your heart. Exposure is the starting point of transformation.

2. **What you try to cover, God will uncover. But what you uncover, God will cover**.

Transparency before God leads to grace, not judgment.

3. **There is restoration even, after failure.**

Adam and Eve were banished from Eden, but God remained in pursuit of humanity, leading to Jesus—the second Adam—who restores what was lost.

Jesus: Stripped So We Could Be Clothed

Jesus was exposed on the cross, stripped not only of His clothing but of human dignity. The soldiers divided His garments and cast lots for His robe (**see John 19:23–24**). He was publicly humiliated so we could be privately restored.

Isaiah says,

> **"I delight greatly in the Lord; my soul rejoices in my God. For he has clothed me with garments of salvation and arrayed me in a robe of his righteousness, ss a bridegroom adorns his head like a priest, and as a bride adorns herself with her jewels." — Isaiah 61:10 (NIV)**

You may be stripped, but because of Jesus, you are never uncovered before God. His righteousness covers you, not your performance. Your brokenness may be visible, but His grace is greater.

Scriptures for Meditation

- Genesis 2:25

- Genesis 3:7–10
- Genesis 3:21
- Isaiah 61:10
- John 19:23–24
- Hebrews 4:13
- Psalm 32:5
- Romans 8:1

You may be in a place of exposure, but you are not defeated. You are known, seen, and still called by God. He will meet you in your nakedness and clothe you in righteousness, grace, and strength.

CHAPTER 3

LOSS, PAIN, AND THE BREAKING OF PRIDE

There is a kind of pain that doesn't just touch the body—it crushes the soul. It leaves you gasping for breath and begging for answers. But pain, though often uninvited, can become a powerful instructor. When loss strips us bare and pride is shattered into pieces, we are brought face to face with our true selves, and our desperate need for God.

Pain has a way of humbling us. In this chapter, we walk alongside a woman whose pain led to the breaking of her pride and the birth of something greater. Her name is Naomi.

Character Focus: Naomi – The Bitter Woman Who Returned Broken but Blessed

Naomi's story is found in the Book of Ruth. Her journey begins with loss—raw, staggering, irreversible loss.

She and her husband, Elimelek, leave Bethlehem during a famine and settle in Moab, a foreign land. There, she suffers devastating losses: first, her husband dies, then her two sons. She is left alone with two Moabite daughters-in-law and no hope for a future. What started as a temporary solution to hunger turned into a permanent season of sorrow.

> **"Now Elimelek, Naomi's husband, died… After they had lived there about ten years, both Mahlon and Kilion also died, and Naomi was left without her two sons and her husband." — Ruth 1:3–5 (NIV)**

Can you imagine the weight of her grief? A husband, gone. Two sons, gone. Her identity as a wife and mother, stripped. Her plans, her legacy, her dreams—all unraveled in a foreign land.

When Naomi returns to Bethlehem, her pain is so deep that she begs her community not to call her Naomi anymore.

> **"Don't call me Naomi," she told them. "Call me Mara, because the Almighty has made my life very bitter." — Ruth 1:20 (NIV)**

The name Naomi means "pleasant," but Mara means "bitter." That's what pain does—it tempts us to rename ourselves by what we've endured. We stop seeing ourselves as God's children and start identifying with our afflictions. We call ourselves broken, bitter, barren, and forgotten.

But what Naomi didn't realize was that while her pride and plans had been stripped, her purpose had not. Her pain became the platform for one of the most beautiful redemptive stories in scripture.

When Pain Strips Away Pride

Pride is subtle. It hides in self-reliance. It disguises itself as strength and independence. But God will often use pain to remove the illusion that we are in control.

Naomi had no choice but to return home empty. And this returning—though humbling—was necessary. She came back to Bethlehem with nothing but a Moabite daughter-in-law named Ruth. What she didn't realize was that this daughter-in-law was the key to restoration.

The Hidden Seed in Your Pain

Sometimes what remains after you've lost everything is the seed of your next season.

> **"So Naomi returned from Moab accompanied by Ruth the Moabite, her daughter-in-law, arriving in Bethlehem as the barley harvest was beginning." — Ruth 1:22 (NIV)**

That last phrase is everything: **"as the barley harvest was beginning."** God brought Naomi back in time for a new harvest. Even when she felt forgotten, He had aligned her return with the start of restoration.

Naomi thought her story was over. But her lineage would soon connect to Boaz and Ruth's marriage, leading directly to King David, and ultimately to Jesus Christ. Naomi's loss positioned her for legacy.

Jesus: Broken for Our Wholeness

Jesus understands the pain of loss and the breaking of pride. In the Garden of Gethsemane, He cried out in agony, surrendering His will to the Father. He bore our grief, carried our sorrow, and was stripped of divine privilege so that we could be made whole.

> **"Surely he took up our pain and bore our suffering… he was pierced for our transgressions, he was crushed for our iniquities… and by his wounds we are healed." — Isaiah 53:4–5 (NIV)**

Pain is not the end. It is a passage. And God doesn't waste pain—He transforms it. When pride is broken and our dependence is surrendered, that's when healing and harvest begin.

Lessons from Naomi's Pain

1. **Loss doesn't mean God has left you.**

Even in Moab, God was with Naomi—preserving Ruth, orchestrating redemption.

2. **Pain may strip you of pride, but it prepares you for promise.**

Naomi returned bitter, but she would soon be holding a grandchild of promise in her arms (**see Ruth 4:16–17**).

3. **You are not who your pain says you are.**

Don't rename yourself based on a temporary valley. You are not "Mara." You are still Naomi—pleasant in God's eyes.

Scriptures for Meditation

- Ruth 1:1–5
- Ruth 1:20
- Ruth 1:22
- Ruth 4:13–17
- Isaiah 53:4–5
- Psalm 34:18
- Romans 8:28
- 2 Corinthians 12:9

You may be in a season of loss. You may feel like everything has been taken, and pride has been shattered. But take heart: your breaking is not your burial. It's your birthing place. God is aligning your return with a new harvest. You are stripped, yes, but not defeated.

CHAPTER 4

WHEN PEOPLE WALK AWAY

Being stripped by circumstances is one thing, but being stripped by people is another. When those you loved, trusted, served, or helped turn their backs on you, the pain cuts deep. Rejection has a way of echoing louder than failure. It isn't just the loss of companionship—it's the tearing of covenant.

But what if the walk-away was divine? What if God allowed the departure so you could discover what He put in you when no one else is left standing?

In this chapter, we explore the journey of David, a man abandoned, misunderstood, and betrayed, but ultimately strengthened in the Lord.

Character Focus: David – Forsaken but Favored

David was anointed king while still a shepherd boy (**see 1 Samuel 16:13**), but the path to the throne was anything but smooth. His journey was marked by betrayal, isolation, and abandonment by those he once trusted.

One of the most powerful moments in David's story came during his time in Ziklag, a place of temporary residence while fleeing King Saul. While living there, David and his men returned from battle to find their city burned, and their wives and children taken by the Amalekites.

The same men who had once followed him into battle now turned on him.

> **"David was greatly distressed because the men were talking of stoning him; each one was bitter in spirit because of his sons and daughters." — 1 Samuel 30:6 (NIV)**

Imagine the weight: you've been loyal, you've fought beside them, and now they want to kill you in their pain. These weren't strangers—they were comrades. Brothers. Friends. And in one moment, they were ready to walk away from everything, including you.

But the verse doesn't end there.

> **"But David found strength in the Lord his God." — 1 Samuel 30:6b (NIV)**

When people walk away, God leans in. When human strength runs out, divine strength steps in. David had no one to lean on, but he discovered the only One who never leaves.

God Allows Some Departures

Sometimes God will allow the people you depended on to walk away, not to punish you, but to position you. He needs you to discover the power of depending on Him alone.

When people leave, it may feel like betrayal, but it could also be deliverance. God may be removing voices that would've kept you stuck. He might be clearing your circle to prepare you for a new mantle.

David had to learn how to lead broken, misunderstood, and alone because his next season wouldn't depend on applause or public approval. It would depend on obedience and intimacy with God.

Even Jesus Was Abandoned

Jesus knew the pain of abandonment. On the night of His arrest, His disciples—those closest to Him—scattered.

> **"Then all the disciples deserted him and fled." — Matthew 26:56b (NIV)**

Even Peter, the most outspoken of the disciples, denied Him three times (**see Luke 22:61–62**). And in His most excruciating moment on the cross, Jesus cried out:

> **"My God, my God, why have you forsaken me?" — Matthew 27:46 (NIV)**

The Son of God, stripped of support, alone in His suffering. Yet, it was that very moment that brought the greatest victory for mankind. His loneliness gave birth to our reconciliation.

So, yes, people will walk away. Friends will fail. Loved ones will leave. But God never will.

> **"Though my father and mother forsake me, the Lord will receive me." — Psalm 27:10 (NIV)**

The Hidden Blessing in Rejection

The people who leave are often not equipped to walk into the next season with you. Their vision is limited. Their loyalty is conditional. But what God has for you goes beyond convenience or popularity.

Rejection is sometimes the greatest form of redirection.

Joseph was sold by his brothers. Jesus was betrayed by Judas. Paul was deserted by Demas (**see 2 Timothy 4:10**). But none of them were defeated. Why? Because the One who called them never left.

Lessons from David's Abandonment at Ziklag

1. **You must learn to encourage yourself.**

When there is no choir to sing your praises, you must become your own worship leader. David strengthened himself in the Lord—not in people, not in circumstances.

2. **Don't stay where the fire burned—pursue what was stolen.**

After seeking God, David received this word: **"Pursue them… you will certainly overtake them and succeed in the rescue." — 1 Samuel 30:8 (NIV)**

3. **Rebuilding begins after everyone leaves.**

God restores what was lost. David recovered all, and then some (**see 1 Samuel 30:18–20**). The stripping season was not the end—it was the setup.

Scriptures for Meditation

- 1 Samuel 30:1–6
- Psalm 27:10
- Matthew 26:56
- Matthew 27:46
- 2 Timothy 4:10
- John 6:66–68
- Romans 8:31
- Isaiah 49:15–16

You may be standing in the ashes of what people left behind. But lift your eyes. God is about to show you that His presence is enough. Their absence did not destroy you—it defined you. Let the walk-away make room for the move of God. You are stripped, but not defeated.

CHAPTER 5

FROM GLORY TO GROUND ZERO

To descend from glory to ground zero is one of the hardest transitions in life. It's when the lights dim, the applause stops, and the crowds disappear. It's when success is replaced by silence, prominence by pain, and recognition by rejection. It's the valley between what was and what will be—a place where your calling is questioned and your confidence is crushed.

Ground zero is where everything collapses. But it's also where God begins again.

In this chapter, we follow the powerful and painful journey of Samson, the man who knew glory but found himself stripped, blind, and grinding in humiliation.

Character Focus: Samson – The Glory Carrier Who Lost It All

Samson's birth was announced by an angel. He was a Nazarite from the womb, chosen by God to deliver Israel from the Philistines (**see Judges 13:5**). He was a man of supernatural strength, empowered by the Spirit of God. He tore lions apart, defeated armies with the jawbone of a donkey, and carried the gates of a city on his back.

But Samson's strength was not in his muscles—it was in his consecration. His long hair symbolized a vow to God, a vow of separation. However, Samson began to toy with his calling, compromise his consecration, and give his heart to someone who did not carry his vision.

Delilah didn't kill him—his disobedience did.

> **"After putting him to sleep on her lap, she called for someone to shave off the seven braids of his hair, and so began to subdue him. And his strength left him." — Judges 16:19 (NIV)**

Then came the stripping.

> **"Then the Philistines seized him, gouged out his eyes and took him down to Gaza. Binding him with bronze shackles, they set him to grinding grain in the prison." — Judges 16:21 (NIV)**

The mighty judge of Israel—the man called by God—was now a blind, broken prisoner. No crowds. No miracles. No victories. Just grinding… in the dark.

The Fall from Glory

Samson's story shows us that you can be called and still fall. You can be gifted and still be defeated. You can operate in public glory while privately compromising your walk. But the beautiful truth of

God's mercy is this: failure does not cancel purpose. Consequences may be real, but calling remains.

Samson's greatest moment came after he was stripped.

> **"But the hair on his head began to grow again after it had been shaved." — Judges 16:22 (NIV)**

Even in ground zero, God was preparing a comeback.

God Builds From Ground Zero

Ground zero is where pride dies and purpose resurrects. It's where you're no longer depending on charisma, connections, or confidence. It's where you say, *"Lord, if You don't do it, it won't be done."*

Samson, in his final act, was no longer performing for applause—he was crying out for redemption.

> **"Then Samson prayed to the Lord, 'Sovereign Lord, remember me. Please, God, strengthen me just once more…'" — Judges 16:28 (NIV)**

And God heard his cry. With one final act of strength, Samson pushed against the pillars of the Philistine temple, killing more enemies in his death than he did in his life.

Samson was stripped, yes, but he was not defeated.

When Your Pillars Collapse

Have you ever watched your own pillars fall? The structures you leaned on—the ministry, the marriage, the momentum, the money—all gone. It feels like God has left the building. But often, He is tearing down man-made strength so He can rebuild you on His foundation.

Ground zero is painful. But it is fertile. It is the soil of surrender. It is where God breathes new life into dry bones.

Ezekiel saw a valley full of bones. They were "very dry." But then came a word from God.

> **"So I prophesied as he commanded me, and breath entered them; they came to life and stood up on their feet—a vast army." — Ezekiel 37:10 (NIV)**

If God can rebuild bones, He can rebuild you.

Jesus: From Cross to Resurrection

Jesus Himself went from glory to ground zero. He left heaven's splendor for a manger, then walked the dusty roads of earth only to be stripped, beaten, crucified, and buried.

The crowds that once shouted *"Hosanna"* now cried *"Crucify Him!"* The One who healed multitudes now hung alone between criminals. He descended to the depths of suffering, but it was there that He conquered death.

"He humbled himself by becoming obedient to death—even death on a cross! Therefore God exalted him to the highest place..." — Philippians 2:8–9 (NIV)

Jesus didn't avoid ground zero. He walked through it—and rose in glory.

Lessons from Samson's Fall and Rise

1. **Don't mistake the presence of the gift for the approval of God.**

Gifts can function in seasons of disobedience, but they won't last. Character must match calling.

2. **God can still use your lowest moment for His highest glory.**

Samson's failure became the platform for his greatest act of obedience.

3. **Your hair will grow again.**

What was lost will be renewed. Your strength, anointing, and fire will return—if you repent and surrender.

Scriptures for Meditation

- Judges 16:4–22
- Judges 16:28–30
- Ezekiel 37:1–10
- Psalm 51:17

- Philippians 2:8–9
- Micah 7:8
- Isaiah 61:3
- 2 Corinthians 4:8–9

You may be standing at ground zero, stripped of everything you once leaned on. But take courage: this is not your burial ground—it's your building site. The hair is growing. The breath is returning. The glory will come again. You are stripped, but not defeated.

PART II

THE FIGHT TO KEEP GOING

CHAPTER 6

HOLDING ON WITH NOTHING LEFT

What do you do when your hands are empty, but your heart still believes? When everything around you is gone—hope, strength, support, resources—but something inside whispers, *Don't let go?*

This is the test of faith that doesn't just trust God when He provides, but clings to Him when He's silent. It's the season where your grip weakens, your prayers grow quiet, and your tears become your language.

This chapter introduces us to a woman whose life had been emptied by sorrow and shattered by loss, yet she held on. Her name is the woman with the issue of blood.

Character Focus: The Woman with the Issue of Blood – Desperate but Determined

We are introduced to her in Mark 5:25–34. Her name is never mentioned. We are only told of her condition.

> **"And a woman was there who had been subject to bleeding for twelve years. She had suffered a great deal under the**

> **care of many doctors and had spent all she had, yet instead of getting better she grew worse." — Mark 5:25–26 (NIV)**

Twelve years. That's more than 4,000 days of bleeding. Of being considered unclean. Of isolation. Of rejection. Of spending everything she had and seeing no results. The Bible says she had nothing left—physically, emotionally, financially, socially.

But she still had faith.

> **"When she heard about Jesus, she came up behind him in the crowd and touched his cloak, because she thought, 'If I just touch his clothes, I will be healed.'" — Mark 5:27–28 (NIV)**

This is what holding on with nothing left looks like. It's not loud. It's not glamorous. It's not posted on platforms. It's a silent, internal decision: I've lost everything, but I refuse to lose my reach for Jesus.

The Reach of the Broken

This woman didn't walk up to Jesus with pride or strength. She crawled, broken and bleeding, through a crowd that had written her off. She was not supposed to be there. She risked stoning, ridicule, and public shame, but her desperation outweighed her fear.

Sometimes, God allows us to be stripped of everything else so that we finally stretch for Him.

And when she touched Him, something happened.

> **"Immediately her bleeding stopped and she felt in her body that she was freed from her suffering." — Mark 5:29 (NIV)**

Her private reach triggered a public miracle. Jesus stopped the crowd. He didn't let her go unnoticed. He wanted to make sure she knew: *It wasn't just the touch—it was your faith that healed you.*

> **"Daughter, your faith has healed you. Go in peace and be freed from your suffering." — Mark 5:34 (NIV)**

What Do You Do When You're Empty?

Many are walking through life spiritually hemorrhaging. You're exhausted from fighting, from believing, from trying to hold everything together. And like this woman, maybe you've been misdiagnosed, mistreated, misunderstood.

But hear this: God doesn't need your strength—He responds to your faith.

> **"Though he slay me, yet will I hope in him…" — Job 13:15a (NIV)**

Faith at the end of yourself is still faith. Holding on by a thread is still holding on. God is not looking for perfection—He is looking for persistence.

When All You Have Is a Thread

This woman didn't grab Jesus—she barely brushed the edge of His garment. And that was enough.

Sometimes, your reach doesn't feel powerful. It may be a whisper of a prayer. A sigh in the night. A tear that says, *God, help me.* That is enough for Jesus to respond.

Jesus said:

> **"If you have faith as small as a mustard seed… nothing will be impossible for you." — Matthew 17:20 (NIV)**

God honors the little you have when it's surrendered to Him. You don't need a full hand—just a willing heart.

Jesus: Holding On in the Garden

Even Jesus had to hold on with nothing left. In the Garden of Gethsemane, He cried out in agony:

> **"My soul is overwhelmed with sorrow to the point of death…" — Matthew 26:38 (NIV)**

He prayed, **"If it is possible, take this cup from me…"** but He held on, choosing surrender: **"Yet not my will, but Yours be done" (see Matthew 26:39).**

This was not weakness—it was obedience in the middle of deep anguish.

Jesus knows what it means to feel pressed, crushed, and abandoned. And He also shows us what it means to endure for the joy set before us (**see Hebrews 12:2**).

Lessons from the Woman with Nothing Left

1. **Your condition doesn't cancel your connection.**

Society called her unclean, but her faith gave her access to Jesus.

2. **Faith isn't always loud—it's often a quiet crawl in the dark.**

She didn't have to shout; she just had to reach.

3. **Healing often comes after everything else is stripped.**

When you've tried everything else, Jesus is still enough.

Scriptures for Meditation

- Mark 5:25–34
- Job 13:15
- Matthew 26:36–39
- Hebrews 12:2
- Isaiah 40:29
- Psalm 34:18
- Romans 4:20–21
- Lamentations 3:22–23

You may be down to nothing, but Jesus is still passing by. Reach, even if it's with trembling fingers. Crawl, even if you're weak. Whisper, even if your voice is gone. Because faith doesn't have to be loud—it just has to be real. You are stripped, but not defeated.

CHAPTER 7

THE BATTLE IN THE MIND

There is no battlefield more persistent, personal, and powerful than the one between your ears. The mind—where thoughts live, memories linger, and fears shout louder than faith—is often the fiercest battleground in your stripping season. You may be stripped externally, but the real war is internal.

It's not what's happening to you that defeats you—it's what's happening in you.

This chapter brings us face to face with a prophet who knew the heights of glory and the depths of mental warfare. His name is Elijah.

Character Focus: Elijah – The Victorious Prophet Who Wanted to Die

Elijah was not just any prophet—he was a fire-caller, rain-stopper, miracle-working servant of God. In 1 Kings 18, he faced down 450 prophets of Baal on Mount Carmel in one of the most dramatic spiritual showdowns in history.

> **"Then the fire of the Lord fell and burned up the sacrifice..." — 1 Kings 18:38 (NIV)**

This moment was glorious. Elijah had proven that Yahweh was the true God. Rain finally came after years of drought. Revival seemed near.

But then, Jezebel sent a message: *You're a dead man.*

> **"So Jezebel sent a messenger to Elijah to say, 'May the gods deal with me... if by this time tomorrow I do not make your life like that of one of them.'" — 1 Kings 19:2 (NIV)**

And just like that, the fire-caller fled in fear. He ran into the wilderness and sat under a broom tree—stripped of courage, emotionally overwhelmed, and mentally tormented.

> **"He came to a broom bush, sat down under it and prayed that he might die. 'I have had enough, Lord,' he said. 'Take my life...'" — 1 Kings 19:4 (NIV)**

This was not just exhaustion. This was a mental collapse. Elijah had hit a wall.

When the Mind Becomes the Battleground

It often happens after the high moments—after the big victories, answered prayers, or visible breakthroughs. Suddenly, anxiety strikes. Fear creeps in. Thoughts spiral out of control. And like Elijah, you go from calling down fire to wanting to disappear.

You can be powerful and still be under pressure. You can be anointed and still feel overwhelmed.

Elijah wasn't weak—he was human. And God didn't rebuke him for his mental struggle. He responded with care.

God's Response to the Weary Mind

1 Kings 19 shows us something profound. God didn't shout. He didn't scold. He didn't condemn Elijah's depression or fear.

Instead, He sent an angel.

> **"All at once an angel touched him and said, 'Get up and eat.'" — 1 Kings 19:5 (NIV)**

Elijah needed rest. Nourishment. Care. He needed to be reminded that his humanity was not a hindrance to his calling.

After he ate and rested, the angel returned again (v. 7). Then God led him to Mount Horeb, where Elijah encountered not thunder or fire, but a still, small voice.

> **"And after the fire came a gentle whisper." — 1 Kings 19:12 (NIV)**

Sometimes when your mind is at war, what you need most is not noise but stillness.

Jesus and the Garden of Mental Warfare

Jesus also fought a mental and emotional battle before His crucifixion. In Gethsemane, His soul was **"overwhelmed with sorrow to the point of death" (see Matthew 26:38).** He prayed so intensely that His sweat became like drops of blood (**see Luke 22:44**).

Yet, He submitted His mind to the will of the Father. He said:

> **"…not my will, but yours be done." — Luke 22:42 (NIV)**

Jesus overcame in the garden so He could overcome at the cross. The battle in the mind comes before the victory in the natural.

Winning the War in Your Thoughts

Paul teaches us how to confront mental strongholds:

> **"We demolish arguments and every pretension that sets itself up against the knowledge of God, and we take captive every thought…" — 2 Corinthians 10:5 (NIV)**

You must capture negative, fearful, or tormenting thoughts and replace them with truth. Your victory doesn't come from feeling better—it comes from believing better.

> **"Do not conform to the pattern of this world, but be transformed by the renewing of your mind." — Romans 12:2 (NIV)**

Renewal isn't instant. It's daily. It's soaking in God's Word, silencing outside voices, and surrendering every anxious thought to the Prince of Peace.

Practical Steps for the Battle in the Mind

1. **Rest.**

Elijah slept and ate. Never underestimate the power of physical rest for mental clarity.

2. **Be honest with God.**

Elijah said, **"I've had enough."** Jesus said, **"Let this cup pass."** God can handle your truth.

3. **Silence the noise.**

Seek God in stillness. The whisper carries more power than the wind.

4. **Get out of isolation.**

God told Elijah to anoint Elisha—a companion for the next season (**see 1 Kings 19:16**). You're not meant to fight alone.

Scriptures for Meditation

- 1 Kings 19:1–13
- Matthew 26:36–39
- 2 Corinthians 10:5
- Romans 12:2
- Isaiah 26:3
- Philippians 4:6–8
- Psalm 42:11
- Lamentations 3:21–23

You may be under mental attack. You may be fighting thoughts that don't align with truth. But let me remind you: *God is not absent in your darkness. He whispers in it.* The enemy wants your mind because he knows that's where your victory begins. But today, renew it. Refuse to be ruled by fear, anxiety, or despair. You are stripped, but not defeated.

CHAPTER 8

SILENCE, SHAME, AND SOLITUDE

There is a kind of silence that deafens you. A silence that speaks louder than words—a stillness that presses on your chest and whispers accusations to your soul. When you've been stripped, silence often moves in. Shame follows closely, wrapping around your heart like a heavy chain. Solitude becomes your new companion, but not the comforting kind—it's the isolating kind that makes you feel forgotten, unseen, and disqualified.

But even here—in the silence, shame, and solitude—God is present. And He does His deepest work, not in the noise, but in the stillness.

In this chapter, we walk with a man who knew the pain of silence, shame, and separation from God's presence: Peter, the disciple who denied Jesus.

Character Focus: Peter – The Disciple Who Denied, Wept, and Was Restored

Peter was bold, passionate, outspoken, and fiercely loyal to Jesus—or so he thought. He declared with confidence:

> **"Even if all fall away on account of you, I never will." — Matthew 26:33 (NIV)**

But Jesus knew better.

> **"Truly I tell you," Jesus answered, "this very night, before the rooster crows, you will disown me three times." — Matthew 26:34 (NIV)**

Peter refused to believe it. But fear doesn't ask for your permission. And when the pressure came, Peter cracked.

> **"Then he began to call down curses, and he swore to them, 'I don't know the man!' Immediately a rooster crowed." — Matthew 26:74 (NIV)**

> **"Then Peter remembered… And he went outside and wept bitterly." — Matthew 26:75 (NIV)**

Can you feel the silence in that moment? The shame in Peter's bitter tears? The solitude in his regret?

Peter—the one who walked on water, saw the transfiguration, and declared Jesus the Christ—had now denied Him publicly. And after that moment, we hear nothing more from Peter during the crucifixion. He fades into the background, overtaken by grief and guilt.

The Silence After Failure

Silence can be torturous after a public fall. When the applause stops and all you hear are whispers, your mind becomes a courtroom and your shame the prosecutor. Every moment replays. Every word echoes. And Satan—who tempted you into the fall—now accuses you in it.

Peter didn't just fail. He failed loudly. And silence settled in afterward—not just around him, but within him.

But God does not leave us in silence. Jesus had already seen Peter's fall coming—and had prepared for it.

> **"But I have prayed for you, Simon, that your faith may not fail. And when you have turned back, strengthen your brothers." — Luke 22:32 (NIV)**

Even before Peter denied Him, Jesus had declared that Peter would return. The silence of shame wasn't Peter's final chapter.

Jesus Breaks the Silence

After the resurrection, Jesus sought Peter out—not to scold him, but to restore him.

In John 21, Jesus cooked breakfast for His disciples. He didn't confront Peter with condemnation—He invited him into a conversation of restoration.

> **"Simon son of John, do you love me?" "Yes, Lord," he said, "you know that I love you." Jesus said, "Feed my lambs." — John 21:15 (NIV)**

Jesus asked Peter this question three times, mirroring the three denials. With each affirmation of love, Jesus restored what shame had shattered. The silence broke. The shame lifted. The solitude ended.

The Power of Divine Restoration

Shame wants to silence you. Solitude wants to convince you that you're disqualified. But grace has another word: *restored.*

Peter went on to preach the gospel boldly on the Day of Pentecost, and 3,000 souls were saved (**see Acts 2:41**). The man who once wept in shame would now lead a revival.

That's what God does in silence—He rebuilds your voice.

Jesus: Alone in Shame and Silence

Even Jesus experienced silence and shame. On the cross, He cried:

> **"My God, my God, why have you forsaken me?" — Matthew 27:46 (NIV)**

The silence of heaven pierced His soul. But that moment wasn't abandonment—it was identification. He took our shame, carried our silence, bore our isolation—so that we could be restored.

> **"He was despised and rejected… a man of suffering… like one from whom people hide their faces." — Isaiah 53:3 (NIV)**

Because He faced ultimate separation, we will never be separated again.

Lessons from Peter's Silence and Restoration

1. **Failure doesn't have to be final.**

Jesus knew Peter's weakness and still called him.

2. **Shame is a liar.**

It says you're done, forgotten, unworthy. But Jesus says you're loved, called, and useful.

3. **Restoration is always personal.**

Jesus came for Peter specifically. He comes for you too.

Scriptures for Meditation

- Matthew 26:33–75
- Luke 22:31–32
- John 21:15–19
- Isaiah 53:3–5
- Romans 8:1
- Psalm 34:5
- Hebrews 4:15–16
- Joel 2:25–27

You may be walking through a silent season. You may be weeping like Peter, convinced that your mistake was the end. But Jesus is already standing on the shore of your life, calling you back—not to punish you, but to restore you. He will break the silence, lift the shame, and end the solitude. You are stripped, but not defeated.

CHAPTER 9

LEARNING TO TRUST AGAIN

One of the most painful results of being stripped is the fracture it causes in your ability to trust. After betrayal, loss, failure, or deep disappointment, trust doesn't return easily. When you've been abandoned by people, failed by systems, or hurt in the house of God, your heart puts up walls to protect itself. You become guarded. Suspicious. Skeptical. And yet, healing doesn't truly begin until you learn to trust again—first in God, then in others, and even in yourself.

Trust is not rebuilt in the absence of pain but in the presence of a God who proves faithful, even when everything else has failed.

In this chapter, we walk with Thomas, the disciple often remembered by his doubt, but whose story speaks to every heart learning how to trust again after being stripped by disappointment.

Character Focus: Thomas – The Wounded Believer Who Needed to See

Thomas was one of the twelve disciples, loyal and faithful to Jesus. He had left everything to follow the Messiah. But like the others, his world was shattered at the crucifixion. Jesus had died—stripped, beaten, and buried—and with Him, Thomas's trust died too.

After Jesus rose from the dead and appeared to the other disciples, Thomas wasn't there. When they told him about the resurrection, he didn't rejoice. He couldn't believe it.

> **"Unless I see the nail marks in his hands and put my finger where the nails were… I will not believe." — John 20:25 (NIV)**

This wasn't just stubbornness—this was trauma. Thomas had seen the crucifixion. The blood. The nails. The lifeless body. He had watched his Teacher die, and now he was being told to hope again? Believe again?

Sometimes, our wounds make us reluctant to trust. And when faith has been pierced, we reach for proof.

Trust After Trauma

Many of us are like Thomas. We want to believe. But the pain of what we saw—what we lived through—has left us cynical. We've been disappointed before. We've been lied to, misled, and let down. And so, our hearts whisper, *"Not again. I won't believe again until I can be sure I won't get hurt again."*

But healing doesn't come through certainty. Healing comes through encounter.

Jesus didn't rebuke Thomas for doubting. He met him in it.

> **"Though the doors were locked, Jesus came and stood among them and said, 'Peace be with you!' Then he said to**

> **Thomas, 'Put your finger here; see my hands… Stop doubting and believe.'" — John 20:26–27 (NIV)**

What love. What mercy. Jesus showed up just for Thomas. He knew the wound that was keeping Thomas from trusting again, and He invited him to touch the very scars that proved not only His pain, but His victory.

God Understands the Struggle to Trust

God knows that trust doesn't rebuild overnight. He's not intimidated by your questions. He's not offended by your honesty. If you are struggling to trust again—He comes not to condemn, but to confirm His presence.

> **"The Lord is close to the brokenhearted and saves those who are crushed in spirit." — Psalm 34:18 (NIV)**

Just as He came for Thomas, He will come for you. He will walk through the locked doors of your heart and offer peace where there was pain.

Learning to Trust Others Again

Not only must we trust God again—we must learn to trust people again. That can be even harder. People fail. People betray. People leave. But not every person is your past. Not every leader is the one who hurt you. Not every friend will abandon you.

Learning to trust again is risky. It opens you to the possibility of being hurt. But it also opens you to the possibility of love, community, healing, and support.

Even Jesus, after being betrayed by Judas, still restored Peter. He still empowered the disciples. He still entrusted His mission to flawed humans. Why? Because love always takes the risk to trust again.

Learning to Trust Yourself Again

Sometimes the greatest mistrust is not with others, but with ourselves. When we've made mistakes, missed signs, fallen for lies, or gone against God's voice, we feel like we can't even trust our own discernment anymore.

But God is a restorer of identity.

Peter denied Jesus, but was restored and commissioned. Moses killed a man, but was still chosen to lead. David committed adultery and murder, but was still called a man after God's heart.

God doesn't throw people away—and neither should you. If He still trusts you with purpose, then you can learn to trust the process of your restoration.

Jesus: Trusting in Gethsemane and Golgotha

Jesus Himself walked the path of stripped trust. In Gethsemane, He prayed, **"Not my will, but Yours."** On the cross, He declared:

> **"Father, into your hands I commit my spirit." — Luke 23:46 (NIV)**

That is trust. Even when everything looks dark. Even when betrayal is fresh. Even when pain surrounds you. He entrusted Himself fully into the Father's hands—and so can you.

Lessons from Thomas and the Journey of Trust

1. **God is not afraid of your doubt.**

He will meet you where you are and invite you to encounter His presence.

2. **Healing begins with honesty.**

Thomas voiced his pain. That's what led to his restoration.

3. **Faith is not the absence of fear—it is the decision to trust in the presence of fear.**

Trust grows when we say, *"God, I don't understand—but I still believe."*

Scriptures for Meditation

- John 20:24–29
- Psalm 34:18
- Isaiah 43:2
- Proverbs 3:5–6
- Romans 15:13
- Luke 23:46
- Jeremiah 17:7
- Psalm 37:3–5

You may be hesitant. Wounded. Cautious. But you are not defeated. Your trust may be fragile, but it's still alive. And if all you have is a whisper of faith, that is enough for Jesus to come close. He will show you His scars to heal yours. You are stripped, but not defeated.

CHAPTER 10

THE POWER OF TEARS AND TRANSPARENCY

Tears are not a sign of weakness—they are evidence that your soul still feels. They are the language of the stripped. When words run dry and strength fades, tears speak. Heaven understands them, and God bottles every one of them as sacred.

Transparency, like tears, often flows from brokenness. In a world that rewards performance and punishes vulnerability, it takes courage to be real. But when you've been stripped, pretending is no longer an option. You've cried enough. You've hidden long enough. And now, healing begins through transparency.

In this chapter, we encounter a woman who brought her tears, her truth, and her treasure to the feet of Jesus: the woman with the alabaster jar.

Character Focus: The Woman with the Alabaster Jar – Broken but Bold

Luke 7 introduces us to a woman known not by name, but by her reputation.

> **"A woman in that town who lived a sinful life learned that Jesus was eating at the Pharisee's house..." — Luke 7:37 (NIV)**

Everyone knew what she had done. No one knew who she really was. But something in her spirit compelled her to press through the crowd, ignore the whispers, and bring her heart—her transparent, messy, unfiltered heart—to Jesus.

She brought an alabaster jar filled with expensive perfume. This wasn't just oil—this was her treasure. Likely her dowry or life savings. And she broke it at Jesus' feet.

> **"As she stood behind him at his feet weeping, she began to wet his feet with her tears. Then she wiped them with her hair, kissed them and poured perfume on them." — Luke 7:38 (NIV)**

What a picture: *weeping, wiping, worshiping.* She had nothing to prove—only love to offer.

While others saw her past, Jesus saw her heart.

The Ministry of Tears

Tears are not random—they are prophetic. They carry your pain, prayers, and surrender. In scripture, tears often preceded deliverance:

- Hannah wept bitterly before conceiving Samuel (**see 1 Samuel 1:10**).

- David wrote psalms of anguish, pouring out his soul to God (**see Psalm 6:6–9**).

- Jesus Himself wept at Lazarus' tomb (**see John 11:35**) and over Jerusalem (**see Luke 19:41**).

Your tears may feel unnoticed, but they are heard in heaven.

> **"You keep track of all my sorrows. You have collected all my tears in your bottle." — Psalm 56:8 (NLT)**

God does not waste tears. He transforms them.

The Weight of Transparency

Transparency doesn't mean sharing everything with everyone, but it does mean being honest before God. It means dropping the act. It means allowing the cracks in your vessel to expose what's real.

The woman with the alabaster jar didn't come with a script or self-defense. She came as she was: broken, sinful, desperate, and unashamed in her expression.

Jesus didn't flinch. He didn't reject her. He received her.

> **"Therefore, I tell you, her many sins have been forgiven—as her great love has shown." — Luke 7:47 (NIV)**

Transparency doesn't repel Jesus—it draws Him closer. He responds not to the polish of our presentation but to the purity of our surrender.

God's Response to the Brokenhearted

God is not searching for perfect people. He's drawn to broken hearts.

> **"The Lord is close to the brokenhearted and saves those who are crushed in spirit." — Psalm 34:18 (NIV)**

> **"A broken and contrite heart you, God, will not despise." — Psalm 51:17 (NIV)**

Tears and transparency prepare the soil of your heart for healing. When you are honest before God, healing flows. And when you stop hiding, shame loses its grip.

Jesus: Transparent in Gethsemane, Weeping at Calvary

Even Jesus allowed tears to fall. In Gethsemane, He sweated drops of blood as He cried out to the Father. On the cross, He was fully exposed—stripped, beaten, bleeding—for all to see. That was not just physical stripping. It was divine transparency.

> **"For we do not have a high priest who is unable to empathize with our weaknesses…" — Hebrews 4:15a (NIV)**

Because Jesus wept, we can weep in His presence without shame.

The Alabaster Moment: What Will You Break?

The woman's alabaster jar was costly, but she broke it willingly because Jesus was more valuable than what she was holding.

Tears + transparency + surrender = transformation.

What are you holding tightly that God is asking you to pour out at His feet? Your plans? Your past? Your pain? That jar isn't meant to be kept—it's meant to be broken in worship.

Lessons from the Alabaster Woman

1. **Tears are spiritual warfare.**

They break strongholds that pride and performance cannot.

2. **Transparency invites divine intimacy.**

God moves where hearts are open.

3. **Brokenness births beauty.**

She entered a sinner. She left forgiven and free.

Scriptures for Meditation

- Luke 7:36–50
- Psalm 56:8
- Psalm 34:18
- 1 Samuel 1:10
- Psalm 51:17

- Hebrews 4:15
- John 11:35
- Romans 8:26

Don't be afraid to cry. Don't be ashamed to be real. Your tears are not your undoing—they are your offering. Your transparency is not your weakness—it is your bridge to healing. At the feet of Jesus, you are seen, loved, and made whole. You are stripped, but not defeated.

PART III

STANDING IN THE MIDDLE OF THE RUINS

CHAPTER II

STRIPPED BUT STILL BREATHING

There comes a moment in your journey where you may not feel strong, but you realize—you're still breathing. And that breath, though it may be shaky, is proof: you're still here. You've been stripped of so much. The loss was real. The betrayal broke something in you. The shame tried to silence you. But here you are—wounded, weary, maybe even wondering—but still breathing.

Breath is life. And in God's hands, your breath is not just survival—it's preparation for revival.

In this chapter, we follow the journey of Ezekiel as he walks through a valley not of victory, but of dry, scattered, lifeless bones.

Character Focus: Ezekiel – The Prophet in the Valley of Bones

Ezekiel was a prophet called to speak during a time of exile, confusion, and spiritual collapse. In Ezekiel 37, God led him to a vision—a valley filled with bones.

> **"The hand of the Lord was on me... He led me back and forth among them, and I saw a great many bones on the floor of the valley, bones that were very dry." — Ezekiel 37:1–2 (NIV)**

Not just bones—very dry bones. Lifeless. Stripped. Scattered. Forgotten.

God then asked a question that speaks to the core of our stripped seasons:

> **"Son of man, can these bones live?" — Ezekiel 37:3 (NIV)**

What a question. When everything looks dead—when the dream is gone, the marriage is ruined, the ministry is empty, and your strength is spent—can it live again?

Ezekiel answered wisely:

> **"Sovereign Lord, you alone know." — Ezekiel 37:3b (NIV)**

When you're standing in a valley of everything you lost, only God can answer that question. But here's the miracle: *God tells Ezekiel to prophesy.*

> **"Prophesy to these bones and say to them, 'Dry bones, hear the word of the Lord!'" — Ezekiel 37:4 (NIV)**

Even in the valley, the bones heard something. And they responded to the word.

Breath Returns in the Broken Place

As Ezekiel obeyed and spoke the Word of the Lord, bones rattled. Flesh appeared. But there was still no breath—no life—until he prophesied again.

> **"So I prophesied as he commanded me, and breath entered them; they came to life and stood up on their feet—a vast army." — Ezekiel 37:10 (NIV)**

This is you. You may feel like scattered bones right now, but there is still a Word over your life. And as long as God's breath exists, your situation is not final.

You may be stripped—but you're still breathing. And that breath is a signal that resurrection is coming.

The Meaning of Breath in Scripture

Breath is not a casual concept in the Bible. It is sacred.

- In Genesis 2:7, God breathed into Adam and he became a living being.
- In John 20:22, Jesus breathed on His disciples and said, **"Receive the Holy Spirit."**
- In Job 33:4, we read: **"The Spirit of God has made me; the breath of the Almighty gives me life." (NIV).**

When the breath of God comes, what was dead lives again. Breath is not just oxygen—it's divine power.

So if you're still breathing, you're still a candidate for resurrection.

Jesus: Breathless on the Cross, but Raised in Power

Jesus, too, was stripped—of His clothing, His dignity, His followers, and finally, His breath.

> **"Jesus called out with a loud voice, 'Father, into your hands I commit my spirit.' When he had said this, he breathed his last." — Luke 23:46 (NIV)**

But three days later, breath returned. Death could not hold Him. The tomb could not trap Him. And because He rose, you will rise too.

> **"The Spirit of God, who raised Jesus from the dead, lives in you." — Romans 8:11 (NLT)**

Your breath is borrowed resurrection power. What you're going through now may have stripped you, but resurrection is breathing on you.

The Significance of Still Breathing

1. **Breath means you're not finished.**

If God was done, you would have stopped breathing. The fact that you woke up today is evidence that there is still purpose.

2. **Breath means prophecy is still in motion.**

God spoke over your life before the stripping—and His Word is still working.

3. **Breath means God is near.**

You may feel far from Him, but if you can inhale, you are inhaling mercy. Each breath is a whisper: *"I'm not done with you yet."*

Lessons from the Valley of Dry Bones

- **Dry doesn't mean dead.**

The bones were very dry, but they still listened. Don't let your dryness convince you that you're disqualified from revival.

- **Sometimes resurrection starts with rattling.**

Things may feel chaotic before they feel complete. That's part of the process.

- **Obedience opens the atmosphere.**

Ezekiel didn't create the miracle. He obeyed God's command to speak. Your obedience—your "yes" in a valley—unlocks revival.

Scriptures for Meditation

- Ezekiel 37:1–10
- Genesis 2:7
- John 20:22
- Romans 8:11
- Job 33:4
- Luke 23:46
- Psalm 150:6
- Isaiah 42:5

You may not have much left. Your resources may be gone. Your strength may be spent. But as long as there is breath in your lungs, there is hope in your future. Breath means God is still working. Breath means resurrection is near. You are stripped, but you're still breathing. And that means—you are not defeated.

CHAPTER 12

WORSHIP IN THE WILDERNESS

Wilderness seasons are some of the loneliest, most disorienting times in a believer's life. They are dry, barren, and confusing places where it seems like the presence of God is distant and the promises of God are delayed—the wilderness strips away comfort, familiarity, and control. But there is something sacred about the wilderness—it teaches you to worship when nothing makes sense.

Worship in the wilderness is not performance. It's not based on circumstances. It's pure surrender. And when everything is gone—when you're stripped of results, rewards, and reassurance—worship becomes your only weapon.

In this chapter, we walk with Hagar, a woman who found herself cast out, abandoned, wandering in the wilderness with nothing, but who discovered that God sees her there.

Character Focus: Hagar – The Forgotten Woman Who Worshiped in the Desert

Hagar was an Egyptian slave, used by Abram and Sarai to produce a child in their impatience with God's promise. She conceived

Ishmael, but tension quickly rose between her and Sarai. Eventually, she was cast out into the wilderness—pregnant, alone, rejected, and wandering.

> **"Then Sarai mistreated Hagar; so she fled from her." — Genesis 16:6 (NIV)**

This is how many of us end up in the wilderness—not by choice, but by rejection. Not because we did something wrong, but because people made decisions that left us discarded. Hagar wasn't just physically lost—she was emotionally crushed.

Yet in that dry, empty place, she had a divine encounter.

> **"The angel of the Lord found Hagar near a spring in the desert…" — Genesis 16:7 (NIV)**

Even in the wilderness, God found her.

The God Who Sees Me

When God speaks to Hagar, He doesn't ignore her pain. He calls her by name, listens to her heart, and reminds her that her child carries a destiny.

Hagar responds with a powerful revelation:

> **"She gave this name to the Lord who spoke to her: 'You are the God who sees me,' for she said, 'I have now seen the One who sees me.'" — Genesis 16:13 (NIV)**

In the wilderness—where she was stripped of status, home, and hope—she discovered God as El Roi, the God who sees. That moment of awareness became an altar of worship. Worship is not always a song—it is a response to revelation. Hagar saw God in the dry place, and it changed her.

Why the Wilderness Is a Holy Place

1. **The wilderness removes distractions.**

There are no crowds. No accolades. Just you and God. In the stillness, you can finally hear His voice.

2. **The wilderness tests the heart.**

Will you still praise when the promise is far away? Will you still trust when the manna doesn't come?

3. **The wilderness reveals provision.**

When Hagar ran out of water, God opened her eyes to a well (**see Genesis 21:19**). Sometimes the provision was always there—you just couldn't see it until worship unlocked your vision.

Worship as Warfare in the Wilderness

You may not feel like singing. Your hands may feel too heavy to lift. But worship is not about how you feel—it's about who God is. And in the wilderness, worship becomes warfare.

- Moses worshiped in the wilderness after the Red Sea split (**see Exodus 15**).
- Israel learned to rely on daily manna in the desert, a lesson in trusting God (**see Exodus 16**).

- Jesus was led by the Spirit into the wilderness and overcame temptation through the Word (**see Matthew 4**).

Worship is not the absence of hardship. It is the declaration of victory in the middle of it.

Jesus: Worshiping Through the Wilderness Journey

Jesus experienced His own wilderness. After His baptism, He was led by the Holy Spirit into a place of testing (**see Matthew 4:1**). For 40 days He fasted, was tempted, and resisted the enemy, not by shouting, but by speaking the Word of God.

Even in the wilderness, He stood firm in worship—placing full dependence on the Father's voice and presence. His example teaches us that wilderness worship isn't emotional—it's intentional.

Worship Doesn't Change the Wilderness—It Changes You

Worship may not immediately shift your surroundings, but it shifts your spirit. You begin to see the wilderness not as punishment, but as preparation. You stop seeing yourself as abandoned and start seeing yourself as chosen—for refinement, for intimacy, for glory.

> **"Even though I walk through the darkest valley, I will fear no evil, for you are with me; your rod and your staff, they comfort me." — Psalm 23:4 (NIV)**

David understood that worship was the anchor. In caves, in deserts, in battle—he worshiped. And so must we.

Lessons from Hagar's Wilderness Worship

1. **God sees you when no one else does.**

Your pain is not invisible. Your wilderness is not ignored. He is El Roi.

2. **Worship is born when you recognize God's presence in unlikely places.**

You don't need a sanctuary—just surrender.

3. **Even in the wilderness, wells still flow.**

If you look through the lens of worship, you'll find water in dry places.

Scriptures for Meditation

- Genesis 16:1–14
- Genesis 21:14–19
- Exodus 15:22–27
- Psalm 63:1
- Matthew 4:1–11
- Psalm 23
- Isaiah 43:19
- Hosea 2:14

You may feel dry. Stripped. Forgotten. But the wilderness is not your grave—it's your meeting place with God. If you will lift your eyes, lift your hands, and lift your heart—He will meet you there.

He sees you. He hears you. And He's preparing a well in the very place that once felt empty. You are stripped, but not defeated.

CHAPTER 13

WHEN FAITH IS ALL YOU HAVE

Faith is beautiful when everything is going well. It's easy to believe when the bank account is full, the diagnosis is clear, the doors are opening, and the blessings are flowing. But the true test of faith is not when you're surrounded by evidence. It's when you have none. It's when the ground has been pulled out from under you, and all you're left with is a whisper in your soul that says, *"Hold on anyway."*

Faith is not the denial of reality. It is the refusal to allow reality to have the final say. And when you are stripped—when you've lost control, comfort, clarity, and confirmation—faith becomes your anchor.

In this chapter, we follow the footsteps of Abraham, the father of faith, who kept walking toward the promise, even when everything around him screamed impossibility.

Character Focus: Abraham – The Man Who Believed Beyond Reason

Abraham had a word from God. It was radical and world-changing: *"You will be the father of many nations."* But the word came to him at a time when he and his wife were well beyond childbearing years.

> **"Against all hope, Abraham in hope believed..." — Romans 4:18 (NIV)**

This was not blind optimism. This was defiant faith—faith that stands in the face of contradiction and says, *"I still believe."*

> **"Without weakening in his faith, he faced the fact that his body was as good as dead... and that Sarah's womb was also dead." — Romans 4:19 (NIV)**

Abraham faced the facts. He wasn't delusional. He acknowledged the circumstances, but he didn't allow them to define God's power. He chose to believe the Word over the wound, the promise over the process.

> **"Yet he did not waver through unbelief... being fully persuaded that God had power to do what he had promised." — Romans 4:20–21 (NIV)**

That's what it means to hold onto faith when it's all you have.

The Stripping That Strengthens Faith

Faith doesn't grow in comfort—it grows in conflict. When you're stripped, your faith either shrinks back or rises up.

- When Job lost everything, he said: **"Though He slay me, yet will I trust in him." — Job 13:15 (KJV)**

- When the three Hebrew boys faced the fiery furnace, they declared: **"Even if He does not deliver us... we will not bow." (see Daniel 3:18).**

That's what mature faith looks like. Not just believing God for something, but trusting God through something.

Faith Is Not a Feeling—It's a Stand

There will be moments in your journey when you feel nothing. The presence of God will seem distant. Prayers will feel unanswered. Circumstances will worsen. But faith is not a feeling—faith is a decision.

> **"Now faith is the substance of things hoped for, the evidence of things not seen." — Hebrews 11:1 (KJV)**

Faith has substance. It holds you up when nothing else can. It is evidence in the courtroom of doubt. It testifies when no one else is present. And it pleases God.

> **"And without faith it is impossible to please God..." — Hebrews 11:6 (NIV)**

God isn't looking for perfect people. He's looking for faith-filled ones—those who keep trusting when the facts look fatal.

Jesus: Faith in the Father Amid Silence and Suffering

Jesus modeled ultimate faith when He hung on the cross. Stripped of dignity, strength, and support, He still trusted.

> **"Father, into your hands I commit my spirit." — Luke 23:46 (NIV)**

In His final breath, He did not cling to outcomes—He clung to the Father. That is faith. And because Jesus modeled it, we can mirror it.

Practical Ways to Strengthen Faith in Stripping Seasons

1. **Feed your faith with the Word.**

Faith comes by hearing, and hearing by the Word of God (**see Romans 10:17**).

2. **Declare the promises of God.**

Speak what He said, even when you can't see it.

3. **Surround yourself with faith-builders.**

Sometimes you need people who will hold up your arms when yours are shaking (**see Exodus 17:12**).

4. **Remember past victories.**

Your history with God is a weapon against current doubt.

Faith in Action: Abraham's Greatest Test

Even after receiving the promised son, Isaac, Abraham's faith was tested again.

> **"Take your son, your only son, whom you love—Isaac—and go to the region of Moriah. Sacrifice him there as a burnt offering on a mountain I will show you." — Genesis 22:2 (NIV)**

What kind of God asks for what He just gave?

But Abraham obeyed. He climbed the mountain with wood and a knife, but also with trust.

> **"We will worship and then we will come back to you." — Genesis 22:5 (NIV)**

Abraham believed that even if Isaac died, God would raise him. That's the kind of faith God is after—not just receiving the promise, but trusting the Promiser regardless.

Lessons from Abraham's Journey of Faith

1. **Faith acknowledges the facts but holds fast to the promise.**

Abraham knew his body was as good as dead, but he didn't let that stop his belief.

2. **Faith is obedience without full understanding.**

Abraham went to a land he didn't know, trusting a God he couldn't see.

3. **Faith can be all you have—and still be enough.**

When stripped of everything else, faith becomes your survival system.

Scriptures for Meditation

- Romans 4:18–21
- Genesis 22:1–18
- Job 13:15
- Daniel 3:17–18
- Hebrews 11:1
- Luke 23:46
- Romans 10:17
- Isaiah 26:3

You may feel like Abraham, walking up a mountain with a knife in one hand and a promise in the other. But faith says: *"God will provide."* You may feel like Job, surrounded by ruins. But faith whispers: *"God still reigns."* You may feel like you're hanging on by a thread, but God says, *"That thread is enough."* You are stripped, but if you still have faith, you are not defeated.

CHAPTER 14

REDISCOVERING IDENTITY WITHOUT THE EXTRAS

One of the most powerful and painful revelations in a season of stripping is this: *You are not your titles.* You are not your position. You are not your possessions. You are not what people think of you. When the extras are gone—the applause, the accomplishments, the affirmations—you are left with your essence. The question becomes: *Do you know who you are without the things that used to define you?*

Stripping forces a confrontation with your true identity. Not the one shaped by culture, accolades, or expectations, but the one authored by God.

In this chapter, we follow the remarkable journey of Joseph, a man who had to lose everything—his coat, his comfort, his status, even his name—before stepping into his true identity.

Character Focus: Joseph – Stripped of the Coat, Covered by Destiny

Joseph was the favored son of Jacob, gifted with dreams and adorned with a coat of many colors—a visible sign of his father's love and his unique destiny.

> **"Now Israel loved Joseph more than any of his other sons… and he made an ornate robe for him." — Genesis 37:3 (NIV)**

That coat represented identity, favor, and calling. But it also stirred jealousy. His brothers hated him, plotted against him, and eventually threw him into a pit. Before they did, they stripped him of his coat.

> **"So when Joseph came to his brothers, they stripped him of his robe… and they took him and threw him into the cistern." — Genesis 37:23–24 (NIV)**

The coat was gone. The dream was intact—but now, it would be tested through betrayal, slavery, lies, and imprisonment.

Stripping Reveals the Strength of Identity

Joseph's identity wasn't in the coat—it was in the call. He was stripped outwardly, but inwardly he remained a man of integrity, vision, and favor.

Even in Potiphar's house as a slave, Joseph excelled. Even in prison after being falsely accused, he interpreted dreams. Even when forgotten, he remained faithful.

He was no longer the "favored son" wearing a robe, but he was still a favored servant of the Most High God. What was on him was removed, but what was in him could not be taken.

Identity Beyond the Extras

Many people build their identity on "extras"—the title before their name, the house they live in, the ministry they lead, the followers they attract. But when the extras are stripped, who are you?

God sometimes allows the stripping to remove every false definition so He can reveal your true foundation—you are who He says you are, even when no one else sees it.

> **"Before I formed you in the womb I knew you, before you were born I set you apart…" — Jeremiah 1:5 (NIV)**

Identity is not discovered in visibility—it's discovered in intimacy with the Father.

Jesus: Stripped of Glory, Secure in Identity

Jesus—the Son of God—was also stripped, not just of His clothes on the cross, but of reputation, recognition, and earthly status.

- Born in a manger, not a mansion.
- Called a carpenter's son, not a king.
- Mocked, misunderstood, and murdered.

Yet throughout His ministry, He constantly affirmed His identity in the Father:

> **"I and the Father are one." — John 10:30 (NIV)**

> **"This is my Son, whom I love; with him I am well pleased." — Matthew 3:17 (NIV)**

Jesus was not moved by opinions, titles, or crowds. His identity was rooted in sonship, not success.

Likewise, your identity must rest in who God says you are, not what life hands you.

From Pit to Palace: Joseph's Promotion Didn't Change His Identity—It Revealed It

Years after being thrown into the pit, Joseph stood before Pharaoh. Not as a victim, not even as a former prisoner, but as a man marked by wisdom, humility, and divine favor.

> **"Then Pharaoh said to Joseph, 'Since God has made all this known to you... You shall be in charge of my palace.'" — Genesis 41:39–40 (NIV)**

Joseph wasn't just restored—he was elevated. But the restoration didn't come from retrieving the robe. It came from living out the dream without needing the symbol to validate it.

Letting Go of What Used to Define You

The stripping season often forces you to let go of former versions of yourself—how people knew you, how you used to operate, what once gave you value. But those things were temporary. What's eternal is this:

"For we are God's handiwork, created in Christ Jesus to do good works, which God prepared in advance for us to do." — Ephesians 2:10 (NIV)

The extras may leave, but you remain. Chosen. Appointed. Anointed.

Lessons from Joseph's Journey of Rediscovered Identity

1. **Losing what's on you does not remove what's in you.**

The coat was symbolic. The calling was spiritual.

2. **God defines you before people recognize you.**

Joseph had dreams before he ever had a position.

3. **You are not who you were—God is forming who you are becoming.**

The pit didn't destroy Joseph. It refined him.

Scriptures for Meditation

- Genesis 37:1–28
- Genesis 39
- Genesis 41
- Jeremiah 1:5
- John 10:30
- Matthew 3:17
- Ephesians 2:10

- Romans 8:16

You may be walking through a season where everything familiar has been removed. The extras are gone. The coat is gone. But your calling is not. Who you truly are is emerging, not the you shaped by people, platforms, or performance, but the one shaped by the hand of God. Don't fight the stripping—embrace the identity that is rising from underneath. You are stripped, but not defeated.

CHAPTER 15

THE GOD WHO SEES YOU NAKED AND STILL CALLS YOU

There's a fear that lingers deep in the human soul: If people really knew me—if they saw me without the masks, the makeup, the ministry—would they still accept me? We've been conditioned to hide flaws, silence weakness, and cover shame. But there comes a point in your journey where you are so stripped—emotionally, spiritually, or even physically—that you have no choice but to stand naked before God, without defense or disguise. And that's where you discover something breathtaking: *He still calls you.* Not after you fix yourself. Not after you rebuild your image. But right there—in your rawest, most vulnerable, most exposed state—He still says, *"You're Mine."*

In this chapter, we walk alongside Adam and Eve, the first humans to be truly seen by God in their nakedness and still covered by His grace.

Character Focus: Adam and Eve – Exposed but Not Erased

In the beginning, Adam and Eve lived in perfect union with God. They were completely exposed, and yet completely unashamed.

> **"Adam and his wife were both naked, and they felt no shame." — Genesis 2:25 (NIV)**

There was no fear in being seen because there was no sin in being known—until one moment of disobedience changed everything.

When Adam and Eve ate from the tree of the knowledge of good and evil, their innocence was shattered.

> **"Then the eyes of both of them were opened, and they realized they were naked; so they sewed fig leaves together and made coverings for themselves." — Genesis 3:7 (NIV)**

Shame entered. And with it, the instinct to hide.

> **"...they hid from the Lord God among the trees of the garden." — Genesis 3:8 (NIV)**

But God didn't leave them there. He came searching.

> **"But the Lord God called to the man, 'Where are you?'" — Genesis 3:9 (NIV)**

This wasn't a question of location—it was a question of condition. God knew where they were. But He wanted them to see where they were. Hiding. Afraid. Stripped of covering, but more importantly, stripped of confidence in His love.

Yet, even then, in their most shameful moment, He didn't stop calling them.

God Sees You and Still Pursues You

You may feel spiritually naked—exposed by sin, by mistakes, by the failures you thought you'd never make. But God is not looking to condemn. He's looking to cover.

> **"The Lord God made garments of skin for Adam and his wife and clothed them." — Genesis 3:21 (NIV)**

Fig leaves were man's attempt to fix the problem. But God knew fig leaves weren't enough. So He sacrificed an animal—a foreshadowing of Jesus—and covered them Himself.

He didn't strip them. He clothed them. He didn't erase their future. He restored their dignity. And He still does the same today.

When You're Naked Before God

Being naked before God means you've stopped pretending. You've stopped performing. You've laid bare every wound, every failure, every dark thought. And in that vulnerability, you find mercy.

> **"Nothing in all creation is hidden from God's sight. Everything is uncovered and laid bare before the eyes of him to whom we must give account. Therefore, since we have a great high priest who has ascended into heaven, Jesus the Son of God, let us hold firmly to the faith we profess. For we do not have a high priest who is unable to empathize with our weaknesses, but we have one who has been tempted in every way, just as we are—yet he did not**

> **sin. Let us then approach God's throne of grace with confidence, so that we may receive mercy and find grace to help us in our time of need." — Hebrews 4:13–16 (NIV)**

You don't have to run. You don't have to hide. The same God who saw Adam and Eve's nakedness and called them is calling you—even now.

Jesus: Stripped on the Cross So You Could Be Covered in Grace

There's no image more sobering than Jesus, the Son of God, stripped on the cross. He wasn't just physically exposed—He was emotionally abandoned, publicly shamed, and spiritually burdened.

> **"When they had crucified him, they divided up his clothes by casting lots." — Matthew 27:35 (NIV)**

He was stripped so we could be covered. He was forsaken so we could be found. And because He stood naked before the wrath of God, we can now stand clothed in the righteousness of Christ.

> **"For he has clothed me with garments of salvation and arrayed me in a robe of his righteousness." — Isaiah 61:10 (NIV)**

You Are Still Called

Your nakedness does not disqualify you. Your exposure does not eliminate your assignment. If God only used the flawless, the Bible would be a pamphlet, not a living book filled with broken people who were still chosen:

- Moses was a murderer, but still called to lead.
- Rahab was a prostitute, but still called into the lineage of Jesus.
- David was an adulterer, but still called a man after God's heart.
- Peter denied Jesus, but still called to preach at Pentecost.

The pattern is clear: *God does not stop calling you just because life has stripped you.*

Lessons from Adam and Eve's Naked Moment

1. **Hiding doesn't heal you.**

Healing begins when you stop hiding and start answering the call.

2. **Your shame does not scare God.**

He already saw it—and still clothed you.

3. **God's covering is better than your fig leaves.**

Let Him robe you in righteousness, not religion.

4. **You are not defined by what you lost, but by the One who found you.**

God is calling you as you are, not as you think you need to be.

Scriptures for Meditation

- Genesis 2:25

- Genesis 3:7–9
- Genesis 3:21
- Isaiah 61:10
- Hebrews 4:13–16
- Matthew 27:35
- Romans 8:1
- 2 Corinthians 5:21

You may feel exposed—stripped of everything that once made you feel confident. But here is the truth that heals: *God sees you. Completely. And He still calls you.* You are not what you've done. You are not what you've lost. You are not what others say. You are who God says you are. You are stripped, but not defeated. And the God who sees you naked still covers you in grace, still calls you by name, and still declares: *"You are Mine."*

PART IV

THE UNSEEN VICTORY

CHAPTER 16

WHAT WAS NOT TAKEN FROM YOU

When you're in a season of loss—when you've been stripped of people, position, peace, or possessions—it's easy to focus on what's missing. The enemy is quick to magnify what you lost so that you overlook what still remains. But here is the truth: *if you still have breath, you still have purpose.* If you still have your faith, your hope, your voice, your God, then you still have everything you need to rise again.

God never allows a stripping that leaves you empty of destiny. What the enemy meant to destroy you has only revealed the things that cannot be taken. This chapter is about rediscovering what still remains and recognizing that what's left is enough to rebuild, to recover, and to rise stronger than before.

To understand this, we walk alongside Paul, a man who lost much but never lost his assignment.

Character Focus: Paul – Persecuted but Preserved

The apostle Paul suffered more than most. Stripped repeatedly of his safety, comfort, freedom, and even his reputation, Paul experienced nearly every kind of loss imaginable.

> **"Five times I received from the Jews the forty lashes minus one. Three times I was beaten with rods, once I was pelted with stones…" — 2 Corinthians 11:24–25 (NIV)**

He was shipwrecked. Imprisoned. Betrayed. Misunderstood. Isolated. Stripped, again and again, by the cost of his calling. Yet Paul never saw himself as a victim—he saw himself as a vessel.

> **"We are hard pressed on every side, but not crushed; perplexed, but not in despair… struck down, but not destroyed." — 2 Corinthians 4:8–9 (NIV)**

Paul learned that no matter how much was taken from him, the most important things remained—his calling, his voice, his anointing, and the abiding presence of God.

Even in prison, stripped of liberty, Paul wrote letters that would change the world.

Even while chained, he still said:

> **"I can do all this through him who gives me strength." — Philippians 4:13 (NIV)**

Shift Your Focus: From What's Lost to What's Left

The enemy wants you to obsess over what you no longer have:

- Who walked away.
- What you failed at.
- What was taken unjustly.

But God wants to show you the residue of glory that still rests on your life. He specializes in working with what's left:

- Moses had a staff and a stutter, but he still had God's call.
- Elijah had depression, but he still had God's voice.
- Job lost everything, but he never lost his relationship with God.
- The widow in 2 Kings 4 had only a small jar of oil, but God used what remained to create overflow.

> **"Tell me, what do you have in your house?" — 2 Kings 4:2 (NIV)**

What do you still have? It might not look like much. But in God's hands, a little is never small.

The Unshakable Things Remain

Hebrews reminds us that some things can be shaken, but some things cannot.

> **"...the removing of what can be shaken... so that what cannot be shaken may remain." — Hebrews 12:27 (NIV)**

Stripping seasons are divine shaking seasons. They reveal the unshakable:

- Your faith.
- Your identity in Christ.
- Your testimony.
- Your eternal hope.

And most importantly, they reveal that God is still with you.

> **"…God has said, 'Never will I leave you; never will I forsake you.'" — Hebrews 13:5 (NIV)**

Jesus: Stripped but Still Savior

On the cross, Jesus was stripped of everything—His garments, His friends, His strength. But He was never stripped of His identity.

He was still the Son of God. Still the Lamb of God. Still the Savior of the world.

And with His final breath, stripped of dignity and life, He declared:

> **"It is finished." — John 19:30 (NIV)**

Not "I am finished"—"It is finished." His assignment was complete. His purpose fulfilled. What man thought was loss was actually victory.

What Was Not Taken From You

When you feel like you've lost everything, remind yourself of what still remains:

- Your mind may be weary, but you still have the mind of Christ (**see 1 Corinthians 2:16**).

- Your body may be tired, but His strength is made perfect in weakness (**see 2 Corinthians 12:9**).

- Your heart may be broken, but God is near to the brokenhearted (**see Psalm 34:18**).

- Your path may be unclear, but the steps of the righteous are ordered (**see Psalm 37:23**).

What remains is more than enough. God can take the ashes of your life and breathe beauty into them.

> **"to give unto them beauty for ashes, the oil of joy for mourning, the garment of praise for the spirit of heaviness;" — Isaiah 61:3 (KJV)**

Lessons from Paul's Stripped Yet Standing Life

1. **You can lose a lot and still keep what matters.**

Faith, favor, and function are not tied to things—they're tied to God's presence.

2. **The anointing doesn't leave when the applause does.**

Paul wrote scripture while forgotten. He wasn't performing—he was obeying.

3. **There is power in what remains.**

God doesn't need what you lost to fulfill what He promised.

Scriptures for Meditation

- 2 Corinthians 4:8–9
- Philippians 4:13
- Hebrews 12:27
- 2 Kings 4:1–7
- Job 1:20–22
- Isaiah 61:3
- John 19:30
- Hebrews 13:5

You may have lost people, platforms, opportunities, but what matters most was never taken from you. God is still with you. His calling is still on your life. His hand is still on your heart. If all you have is your breath and your faith—that's enough. You are stripped, yes, but what remains is more than enough to rebuild. You are not defeated.

CHAPTER 17

BEAUTY IN BROKENNESS

We live in a world that idolizes perfection and hides brokenness. From filtered images to polished sermons, we are conditioned to conceal the cracks in our lives. But in the kingdom of God, brokenness is not a liability—it's a gateway to beauty.

It is in brokenness that we encounter the heart of God. It is in the places of pain, surrender, and tears that we are shaped, purified, and positioned for glory. What the world discards, God redeems. And what man sees as shattered, God sees as a vessel for His light.

This chapter draws from the life of Mary of Bethany, a woman who discovered that brokenness is not the end of usefulness—it is the beginning of worshipful beauty.

Character Focus: Mary of Bethany – The One Who Broke the Jar

Mary of Bethany is known for many things—her posture at Jesus' feet, her tears, her attentiveness—but perhaps most notably, for what she broke.

> **"...a woman came with an alabaster jar of very expensive perfume... She broke the jar and poured the perfume on his head." — Mark 14:3 (NIV)**

This was not an accidental break. This was intentional. It was prophetic. It was costly. Alabaster was a hard, polished stone. To access the fragrance inside, the vessel had to be broken. The moment Mary broke the jar, the aroma filled the room—and her worship filled heaven.

Her brokenness became her beauty. The act of shattering what was valuable symbolized her surrender and devotion to Jesus.

> **"Leave her alone," said Jesus. "Why are you bothering her? She has done a beautiful thing to me." — Mark 14:6 (NIV)**

Jesus called her broken act beautiful. This is the paradox of God's kingdom: broken things, when given to Him, release unmatched glory.

Brokenness Is Not a Curse—It's a Calling

The world tells you to hide your scars. God says, *"Show me where it hurts."* Why? Because He heals what is revealed. And more than that, He uses it.

> **"The Lord is close to the brokenhearted and saves those who are crushed in spirit." — Psalm 34:18 (NIV)**

You don't have to pretend to be whole when you're not. You don't have to act strong when you feel shattered. God specializes in collecting the fragments of your soul and creating something eternal with them.

> **"He heals the brokenhearted and binds up their wounds." — Psalm 147:3 (NIV)**

God's Power Flows Through Cracked Places

In 2 Corinthians 4:7, Paul writes:

> **"But we have this treasure in jars of clay to show that this all-surpassing power is from God and not from us."**

God doesn't place His power in perfect vessels. He uses fragile ones—cracked pots and chipped jars. Why? Because through those cracks, His light shines brightest.

Your brokenness is not your disqualification. It's your distinction. It's what makes your story powerful. Your scars tell a testimony. Your tears water the soil of ministry. Your pain becomes the oil that pours out on others.

Jesus: Broken So You Could Be Healed

The greatest example of beauty from brokenness is Jesus Himself.

> **"But he was pierced for our transgressions, he was crushed for our iniquities; the punishment that brought us peace was on him, and by his wounds we are healed." — Isaiah 53:5 (NIV)**

The body of Jesus was broken—His hands pierced, His side opened, His back torn. He was stripped, beaten, and bruised. But from that brokenness came the beauty of our redemption. The crushing of the Savior became the cure for the sinner.

Communion reminds us of this:

> **"...this is my body, which is broken for you." — 1 Corinthians 11:24 (KJV)**

Brokenness has always been part of God's plan for bringing forth glory. The cross was ugly, but the resurrection was beautiful.

There is Glory in the Cracks

Kintsugi is the Japanese art of repairing broken pottery with gold, making the cracks part of the design rather than something to hide. The break becomes the most beautiful part of the vessel.

That's what God does with us.

- He turns your divorce into a ministry of healing.
- He turns your bankruptcy into wisdom for others.
- He turns your abuse into a voice for the voiceless.
- He turns your loss into compassion for those grieving.

> **"To all who mourn... he will give a crown of beauty for ashes..." — Isaiah 61:3 (NLT)**

The parts of you that you thought disqualified you are the parts God wants to use for His glory.

Lessons from Mary's Broken Alabaster

1. **Breaking releases the fragrance.**

If Mary had kept the jar intact, the scent would've stayed inside. Brokenness released the beauty.

2. **What the world calls waste, Jesus calls worship.**

The disciples criticized her. But Jesus defended her. Don't let man's opinions stop your offering.

3. **God remembers broken offerings.**

"Truly I tell you, wherever the gospel is preached... what she has done will also be told." — Mark 14:9 (NIV)

Your broken story may feel small, but in heaven, it's memorialized.

Scriptures for Meditation

- Mark 14:3–9
- Psalm 34:18
- Isaiah 53:5
- 2 Corinthians 4:7
- Isaiah 61:3
- Psalm 147:3
- Luke 7:37–50
- 1 Corinthians 11:24

Your brokenness is not the end of your story. It's the beginning of your beauty. What shattered you will not stop you. What hurt you will not hinder you. God will take the broken jar of your life, pour out what's left, and call it beautiful. Don't hide your scars—reveal His glory through them. You are stripped. You are cracked. But you are not defeated. You are becoming a vessel of honor—beauty in brokenness.

CHAPTER 18

LESSONS ONLY STRIPPING CAN TEACH

There are some things you cannot learn in a palace. Some truths will never be taught on the mountaintop. Some wisdom is forged only in the wilderness, only in the fire, only in the valley where everything that once held you together has been pulled away.

Stripping is a teacher.

It does not ask permission. It walks into your life uninvited. It dismantles the layers you've built for protection. It forces you to examine the foundation beneath the appearance. But if you pay attention—if you lean in rather than run—you will find that stripping comes with lessons that only it can teach.

In this chapter, we learn from Naomi, a woman who lost everything—husband, sons, homeland—and discovered that while stripping may empty your hands, it can never cancel your destiny.

Character Focus: Naomi – Emptied But Not Erased

Naomi's life began with blessing. She was married, fruitful, and full. But famine led her family to Moab, and there the stripping began. One by one, the things she loved were taken: her husband, Elimelech, and her two sons.

> **"Now Elimelek, Naomi's husband, died… After they had lived there about ten years, both Mahlon and Kilion also died, and Naomi was left without her two sons and her husband." — Ruth 1:3–5 (NIV)**

She returned home bitter, broken, and barren, not only in body but in spirit.

> **"Don't call me Naomi," she told them. "Call me Mara, because the Almighty has made my life very bitter." — Ruth 1:20 (NIV)**

Her name meant pleasant, but her experience now felt like bitterness. Naomi saw herself as stripped, empty, and forgotten. But the stripping wasn't the end of her story—it was the beginning of God's redemptive setup.

Stripping Teaches You to Rely on What Truly Matters

When Naomi lost her family, she still had one thing left: a loyal daughter-in-law named Ruth. And through Ruth, God began to rebuild what was lost.

> **"Where you go I will go, and where you stay I will stay. Your people will be my people and your God my God." — Ruth 1:16 (NIV)**

Naomi was too hurt to see it at the time, but even in her stripping, God had preserved a remnant.

Stripping teaches you to see what remains instead of what was removed.

Five Lessons Stripping Will Teach You

1. **You are not your loss.**

Naomi lost family, but she didn't lose her future. You may have suffered a stripping season, but your losses do not define your legacy. Pain visited her life, but so did Boaz. So did redemption. So did Jesus, who would be born through the very lineage God rebuilt through her daughter-in-law, Ruth.

> **"Boaz was the father of Obed… Obed the father of Jesse, and Jesse the father of David." — Ruth 4:21–22 (NIV)**

2. **There is still purpose in your pain.**

What Naomi thought was an ending was actually an intersection—where pain and purpose met. She became a mentor, a midwife of destiny for Ruth. She guided her to Boaz. She nurtured a promise.

> **"Then Naomi took the child in her arms and cared for him." — Ruth 4:16 (NIV)**

Naomi went from mourner to mother of legacy.

3. **Stripping tests what you truly believe about God.**

Naomi felt like God had turned against her. But He hadn't. He was positioning her for restoration. In the stripping, your faith is tested, but it is also purified.

> **"…when he has tested me, I will come forth as gold." — Job 23:10 (NIV)**

4. **You can be bitter and still be blessed.**

God is not intimidated by your emotions. Naomi said, **"Call me bitter."** God didn't rebuke her. He just kept working. You may feel wounded, angry, or disappointed, but that doesn't disqualify you from what God is doing. Healing is still available. Blessing is still on the way.

5. **What God is building in the background is bigger than what you lost.**

Naomi thought her family line had ended. But God was setting up King David—and eventually, King Jesus. She didn't just survive the stripping—she became a central figure in salvation's story.

Stripping Removes False Security

We often trust in things that feel stable: relationships, income, status, platforms, routines. Stripping removes those comforts and exposes what our hearts have truly been anchored in.

But this is mercy. Why? Because when the false securities are gone, we can rediscover our true foundation:

> **"For no one can lay any foundation other than the one already laid, which is Jesus Christ." — 1 Corinthians 3:11 (NIV)**

Stripping reminds you: *He is enough.*

Jesus: Stripped So We Could Be Made Whole

No one was stripped more than Jesus. He was stripped of friends, stripped of clothing, stripped of strength. On the cross, He even cried out:

> **"My God, my God, why have you forsaken me?" — Matthew 27:46 (NIV)**

But through His stripping came the greatest victory.

> **"...by his wounds we are healed." — Isaiah 53:5 (NIV)**

Stripping, when placed in God's hands, always leads to resurrection.

Lessons from Naomi's Stripping Season

1. **God can rebuild, even when you think it's too late.**

Naomi's restoration came through the next generation, but it was still her story.

2. **You don't need to be strong to be used—you just need to be surrendered.**

Naomi wasn't perfect. But she was present.

3. **Pain doesn't cancel promise—it prepares you for it.**

Naomi's loss made room for Ruth, and Ruth's obedience birthed legacy.

Scriptures for Meditation

- Ruth 1–4
- Job 23:10
- Isaiah 53:5
- Matthew 27:46
- 1 Corinthians 3:11
- Psalm 30:5
- Romans 8:28

Stripping feels like the end, but in God's hands, it becomes a beginning. It teaches what comfort never could. It reveals what surface living always hides. And though it hurts deeply, it births something holy. Naomi lost much, but she gained more. You may feel empty, but God is still writing your next chapter. You are stripped. You may feel forgotten. But you are not defeated. In fact, you're learning what only stripped souls ever learn: *you are stronger than you thought, and God is closer than you knew.*

CHAPTER 19

FROM STRIPPED TO STRENGTHENED

There is a shift that happens after the storm, after the pain, after the stripping. It doesn't come all at once—it begins subtly, silently, in the places where you thought you would remain broken. What started as a season of devastation becomes a testimony of divine strength. You begin to realize: *you are still standing.* You survived what should have destroyed you. You lost much, but gained something greater—you gained spiritual strength.

This is not the strength the world gives. This is not muscle or might. This is the unshakable, immovable kind of strength that comes only through trial, only through pressing, only through the fire of being stripped and still choosing to trust.

This chapter highlights the transformation of Peter, a man who was broken, sifted, and stripped, but who emerged strengthened and made fit for the Master's use.

Character Focus: Peter – Sifted but Standing

Peter, the bold disciple, was known for his passion and confidence. He walked on water. He declared Jesus to be the Son of God. He swore his loyalty, even unto death.

> **"Even if all fall away on account of you, I never will." — Matthew 26:33 (NIV)**

But Jesus knew something Peter didn't—a stripping was coming.

> **"Simon, Simon, Satan has asked to sift all of you as wheat. But I have prayed for you, Simon, that your faith may not fail." — Luke 22:31–32 (NIV)**

Peter didn't understand at the time. But soon, he would be stripped of all the pride and strength he thought he had. He would deny Jesus three times. He would weep bitterly. And he would be left wondering if he had forfeited everything.

But what Peter didn't know was that his sifting would lead to strengthening.

> **"And when you have turned back, strengthen your brothers." — Luke 22:32b (NIV)**

Jesus didn't just predict Peter's failure—He prophesied his return. He saw the strength that would emerge from the stripping.

Sifting Prepares You for Strength

To sift means to shake violently, to separate the grain from the chaff. It is an act of purifying, of removing what is useless to reveal what is valuable. That's what Peter endured—and what many of us experience.

You're not being punished—you're being prepared.

- Stripping removes false confidence.
- Sifting removes impure motives.

- Crushing reveals true dependence on God.

Peter's failure was not his end. It was his beginning. After being restored by Jesus (**see John 21**), Peter became a pillar of the church. He preached at Pentecost. He healed the sick. He stood in boldness where once he ran in fear.

The one who denied Jesus became the one who declared Him to the world.

You Are Stronger Than You Think

It's not that the pain didn't come. It's not that the losses weren't real. It's that God used them to fortify you. And now, you don't just have a testimony—you have spiritual weight. You carry wisdom, discernment, compassion, and courage that you didn't have before.

> **"But those who hope in the Lord will renew their strength. They will soar on wings like eagles…" — Isaiah 40:31 (NIV)**

Strength isn't just about standing tall—it's about learning to stand again after you've fallen.

> **"Though he may stumble, he will not fall, for the Lord upholds him with his hand." — Psalm 37:24 (NIV)**

Jesus: Strength in Stripping

Jesus Himself modeled this. In Gethsemane, stripped of comfort, He prayed, **"Not my will, but yours be done."** He endured the cross, scorning its shame, and emerged with resurrection power.

> **"For he was crucified in weakness, but lives by the power of God." — 2 Corinthians 13:4 (ESV)**

Stripped, but not defeated.

We do not gain power by avoiding pain. We gain power by going through it with God's presence.

From Weeping to Witnessing

Peter's transformation is proof that God doesn't discard the stripped—He restores and reuses them.

- He went from weeping to witnessing.
- From denial to declaration.
- From falling to founding the early church.

God used the failure to build a foundation of strength, grace, and mercy.

Lessons from Peter's Sifting and Strengthening

1. **God prays for your return before your failure begins.**

Jesus interceded for Peter before he ever fell.

2. **Your faith can be refined without being destroyed.**

Sifting is not the end—it's the transformation process.

3. **What breaks you now builds you later.**

Peter's lowest point became his launching point.

4. **Strength is not the absence of weakness—it's the presence of God in your weakness.**

   "My grace is sufficient for you, for my power is made perfect in weakness." — 2 Corinthians 12:9 (NIV)

Scriptures for Meditation

- Luke 22:31–34
- John 21
- Acts 2
- Psalm 37:24
- Isaiah 40:31
- 2 Corinthians 12:9
- 2 Corinthians 13:4
- Philippians 4:13

Stripping did not make you weak. It revealed where your real strength lies. Like Peter, you may have denied, doubted, or despaired, but Jesus never left you. He prayed for you through the sifting. And now, you are not only surviving—you are strengthened. You are wiser, bolder, humbler, and more powerful than before. You are no longer defined by what was stripped. You are defined by who you became through it. You are not defeated. You are rising in strength, clothed in grace, and walking in power.

CHAPTER 20

THE RE-CLOTHING—WHAT GOD PUTS ON YOU AFTER THE STRIPPING

There is a moment after the stripping, after the brokenness, after the tears, when God begins to clothe you again. Not in the garments you once wore—garments of pride, performance, or pain—but in the garments He chooses for you: garments of purpose, power, and purity.

The re-clothing process is often quiet. It happens in the secret place. God takes His time. He doesn't just restore what you lost—He robes you with what is eternal.

The same God who allowed the stripping is the God who initiates the re-dressing. And when God dresses you, it's not just with outward favor—it's with inward transformation. This chapter leads us through this redemptive moment by walking alongside Joseph, a man who was stripped not once—but twice—and yet re-clothed with destiny.

Character Focus: Joseph – Stripped by Man, Robed by God

Joseph's story begins with a coat—a multicolored garment symbolizing his father's favor (**see Genesis 37:3**). But that coat made him a target. His brothers, burning with jealousy, stripped him of it and threw him into a pit.

> **"So when Joseph came to his brothers, they stripped him of his robe—the ornate robe he was wearing—and they took him and threw him into the cistern. The cistern was empty; there was no water in it." — Genesis 37:23–24 (NIV)**

Later, in Potiphar's house, Joseph was again stripped—this time by lies and accusation. Potiphar's wife grabbed his cloak and accused him of assault. Once again, a garment was taken—and once again, he was thrown down, this time into a prison.

But through every stripping, God was preparing Joseph for the robe that really mattered.

After years in a dungeon, Joseph is brought before Pharaoh to interpret a dream. The dream saves Egypt—and suddenly, Joseph is not only restored, he's elevated.

> **"Then Pharaoh took his signet ring... He dressed him in robes of fine linen and put a gold chain around his neck." — Genesis 41:42 (NIV)**

Joseph was re-clothed—not in favoritism, not in accusation—but in authority.

God Doesn't Just Restore—He Redefines

Joseph's first robe was given by a father who favored him. His second robe was ripped away by betrayal. His third robe was bestowed by a king—a king who saw the hand of God on his life.

This is the progression for us too:

1. What man gives can be stripped.
2. What man takes may cause pain.
3. But what God gives—no one can take away.

The re-clothing is not about re-wearing what you lost. It's about stepping into new garments—spiritual clothing that reflects your refined identity.

> **"For he has clothed me with garments of salvation and arrayed me in a robe of his righteousness." — Isaiah 61:10 (NIV)**

You Are Being Re-Clothed

When God re-clothes you, it doesn't always look like fame or favor. Sometimes it looks like:

- Peace in the place where anxiety ruled.
- Joy where sorrow once lived.
- Discernment where confusion dwelled.
- Grace where guilt once held you hostage.

You may not see the robe physically, but heaven has declared: you are robed in righteousness.

Jesus: Stripped So We Could Be Clothed

No one was more violently stripped than Jesus.

> **“They stripped him and put a scarlet robe on him… they took off the robe and put his own clothes on him.” — Matthew 27:28–31 (NIV)**

He was mocked, humiliated, and hung exposed. But His stripping made way for our re-clothing.

> **“for all of you who were baptized into Christ have clothed yourselves with Christ.” — Galatians 3:27 (NIV)**

Now, because of Jesus, you are not wearing shame—you are wearing salvation.

What God Puts on You After the Stripping

1. **The Garment of Praise for the Spirit of Heaviness**

> **“To bestow on them… the oil of joy instead of mourning, and a garment of praise instead of a spirit of despair.” — Isaiah 61:3 (NIV)**

You once wore heaviness like a cloak. But now, God is replacing it with praise.

2. **The Robe of Righteousness**

You are not dressed in your past—you are clothed in Christ’s righteousness.

> **"I delight greatly in the Lord... he has clothed me with garments of salvation." — Isaiah 61:10 (NIV)**

3. **The Armor of God**

You are not naked in battle. You are clothed in power.

> **"Put on the full armor of God, so that you can take your stand..." — Ephesians 6:11 (NIV)**

4. **The Mantle of Ministry**

Like Elijah's cloak passing to Elisha, God will mantle you with purpose again.

You Are Not Who You Were

When God re-clothes you, He also re-names and re-frames you:

- Joseph was no longer the pit-dweller. He became the prime minister.
- Ruth was no longer the widow. She became the wife of Boaz.
- Paul was no longer the persecutor. He became the preacher.
- You are no longer stripped and shamed. You are clothed and called.

> **"...anyone who belongs to Christ has become a new person. The old life is gone; a new life has begun!" — 2 Corinthians 5:17 (NLT)**

Lessons from Joseph's Re-Clothing

1. **Man may strip you of status, but God will robe you with significance.**

What was taken was temporary. What God gives is eternal.

2. **Every stripping is preparing you for a greater re-clothing.**

Joseph's dungeon became his dressing room for destiny.

3. **You're not going back to what you wore—you're stepping into something new.**

The re-clothing isn't a repeat—it's a revelation.

Scriptures for Meditation

- Genesis 37:3–24
- Genesis 41:42
- Isaiah 61:3, 10
- Matthew 27:28–31
- Galatians 3:27
- 2 Corinthians 5:17
- Ephesians 6:10–17
- Zechariah 3:3–5

The stripping was real. The pain was deep. But God never intended for you to stay uncovered. He is the God who clothes you, not just externally, but internally. He puts on you a new vision, new power, new identity. What was torn off is not your ending. What God puts on you now is proof: *You are not defeated.* You are robed in righteousness, covered in grace, armed for battle, and clothed for purpose. The pit could not steal your promise. The prison could not stop your promotion. And the stripping only made room for the new. You are re-clothed—and you are ready.

CHAPTER 21

YOU ARE NOT WHAT WAS TAKEN

When stripping happens—when people walk away, when positions are lost, when dreams are shattered—it's easy to start identifying with what's missing rather than what remains. The trauma of loss can leave you with questions: *Who am I now? Am I still valuable? What's left of me?*

But the truth is this: *you are not what was taken from you.*

- You are not the divorce.
- You are not the layoff.
- You are not the betrayal.
- You are not the death.
- You are not the mistake.
- You are not the shame.

You are who God says you are, and His Word never changes based on what you lose.

This chapter brings us into the journey of Mephibosheth, the grandson of King Saul, who lost everything—but was still remembered by the King of kings.

Character Focus: Mephibosheth – Dropped, Stripped, but Not Forgotten

Mephibosheth was royalty. He was born into a royal lineage. But one tragic day, his nurse fled with him after hearing about the death of his grandfather, Saul, and his father, Jonathan. In her haste, she dropped him, leaving him crippled for life.

> **"He was five years old when the news about Saul and Jonathan came… His nurse picked him up and fled, but as she hurried to leave, he fell and became disabled." — 2 Samuel 4:4 (NIV)**

From that moment, Mephibosheth's life changed. He was stripped of his heritage, his mobility, his royal position, and his identity. He grew up in Lo-Debar—a barren, forgotten place, where broken things go to hide.

Years passed, and Mephibosheth must have believed the lie: This is who I am now. Just a crippled man in hiding. Forgotten. Rejected. Nothing left of the boy I used to be.

But one day, everything changed.

When the King Calls Your Name

David, now king, remembered a covenant he had made with Jonathan, Mephibosheth's father.

> **"Is there anyone still left of the house of Saul to whom I can show kindness for Jonathan's sake?" — 2 Samuel 9:1 (NIV)**

They brought word: There is one—Mephibosheth.

Despite the years, despite the condition, despite the hiding, the King called him by name.

When Mephibosheth appeared before David, he bowed and called himself a "dead dog" (**see 2 Samuel 9:8**). That's what trauma will do—it will make you believe you are less than who you were created to be.

But David didn't see a cripple—he saw a covenant.

> **"Don't be afraid," David said to him, "for I will surely show you kindness... I will restore to you all the land that belonged to your grandfather Saul, and you will always eat at my table." — 2 Samuel 9:7 (NIV)**

You Are Not What Was Taken—You Are What God Remembers

You are not the broken pieces—you are the promise that remains. You are the covenant that God still intends to keep.

Even when others forget you, even when you feel disqualified by your condition, God remembers.

He remembers His Word over your life.

He remembers the prayers you prayed.

He remembers the promise He made.

> **"Can a woman forget her nursing child, and not have compassion on the son of her womb? Surely they may forget, yet I will not forget you." — Isaiah 49:15 (NKJV)**

Your Condition Does Not Change Your Position

Mephibosheth was still crippled.

But now, he sat at the king's table—as one of his sons.

> **"And Mephibosheth lived in Jerusalem, because he always ate at the king's table; he was lame in both feet." — 2 Samuel 9:13 (NIV)**

God does not wait for your condition to be corrected before He restores your position.

You may walk with a limp, but you're still chosen. You may have a past, but you still have a place at the table.

You're More Than the Pain You've Been Through

God never calls you by your limp. He calls you by your name.

He doesn't label you based on what you lost. He marks you based on what He's restoring.

- Joseph wasn't the prisoner. He was the ruler.
- Naomi wasn't Mara. She was still pleasant.
- Rahab wasn't a harlot. She became part of Jesus' lineage.
- Mephibosheth wasn't forgotten. He was invited.

And you? You are not what you've been through. You are not what you've lost. You are what God has planned next.

Lessons from Mephibosheth's Restoration

1. **Your value is not determined by your past or your pain.**

You were royal before the fall—and God still sees royalty in you.

2. **You may have been dropped, but you have not been disqualified.**

Your limp does not eliminate your seat at the table.

3. **You are not hidden from God's memory.**

The King is calling your name, even from Lo-Debar.

4. **What was taken is not greater than what will be restored.**

Mephibosheth received not only a seat but all that belonged to his grandfather, Saul.

Jesus: Redeemer of the Stripped and Broken

Mephibosheth is a prophetic picture of what Jesus does for us:

- We were broken and hiding.
- We were crippled by sin.
- We were living beneath our identity.

But Jesus came, full of grace, calling us back, not based on our merit, but based on covenant love.

> **"While we were still sinners, Christ died for us." — Romans 5:8 (NIV)**

He clothed us. He restored us. And He seated us in heavenly places.

"And God raised us up with Christ and seated us with him in the heavenly realms…" — Ephesians 2:6 (NIV)

Scriptures for Meditation

- 2 Samuel 4:4
- 2 Samuel 9
- Isaiah 49:15
- Romans 5:8
- Ephesians 2:6
- Psalm 139:16
- Jeremiah 29:11
- 1 Peter 2:9

You are not the thing that hurt you. You are not the chapter that stripped you. You are not what they said, not what was stolen, not what you failed at. You are what God says you are. And He says you are still royal. Still seated. Still chosen. Still loved. You are not what was taken—you are what He's about to release. You are not defeated. You are remembered, restored, and rising.

CONCLUSION

FROM STRIPPED TO STRENGTHENED TO SENT

You have walked through the pages of pain.

You have stood in the shadows of sorrow.

You have been stripped—by life, by loss, by betrayal, by disappointment.

But you are still here. And because you are still here, God is not finished.

This book was never meant to glorify the stripping—it was meant to show you what happens after it. It was meant to walk with you through the valley of exposure and help you emerge clothed in purpose, power, and promise. Because stripping was never the destination, it was preparation. It was the fire before the refining. The tearing before the tailoring. The wilderness before the commissioning.

You are not just stripped.

You are strengthened.

And now, you are being sent.

Your Pain Has Become Your Platform

Everything you thought disqualified you was actually making you more qualified. Why? Because now you don't speak from theory—you speak from experience. You know what it's like to fall—and to get back up. You know what it's like to be emptied, and then filled again. You know what it's like to be left alone, and to find out that God never left.

This kind of authority doesn't come from books or pulpits. It comes from the pit. From the prison. From the crushing. And now your voice carries weight. Your scars carry testimony. Your tears carry intercession. And your limp tells the world that you wrestled with God and lived to tell the story.

> **"Blessed is the one who perseveres under trial because, having stood the test, that person will receive the crown of life…" — James 1:12 (NIV)**

God Didn't Just Let You Survive—He's Raising You Up

You didn't make it through all that just to go back to normal. You've been refined for assignment.

- Like Joseph, who went from being stripped in the pit to standing in the palace.
- Like Naomi, who went from bitter to blessed with legacy.

- Like Peter, who went from denying Christ to declaring Him with boldness.

- Like Mephibosheth, who went from hiding to feasting at the King's table.

These stories aren't just ancient—they are prophetic blueprints. They are your reality.

You've moved from:

- Stripped → identity exposed
- Strengthened → identity rebuilt
- Sent → identity activated

You Are Being Sent to Others Who Are Stripped

This journey was not just for you. God is raising you as a voice for the voiceless, a comforter to the crushed, a mentor to the broken.

> **"He comforts us in all our troubles so that we can comfort others…" — 2 Corinthians 1:4 (NLT)**

You are now a midwife to someone else's miracle. A bridge for someone else's breakthrough. A living, breathing testimony that you can lose everything—and still win.

Your story is no longer just about what was taken—it's about what was birthed in you.

A Final Charge to the Stripped-But-Still-Standing One

- Don't let shame keep you from stepping back into purpose.
- Don't let the memory of the stripping silence the message of your healing.
- Don't wear defeat when God has clothed you with destiny.
- Don't walk like a victim when God has anointed you as a vessel.

There is more. More fire. More favor. More fulfillment. More assignment.

The stripping was real, but so is the sending.

You are rising now, not in your own strength but in His.

> **"And the God of all grace, who called you to his eternal glory in Christ, after you have suffered a little while, will himself restore you and make you strong, firm and steadfast." — 1 Peter 5:10 (NIV)**

Scriptures to Seal This Season

- Isaiah 43:2
- 1 Peter 5:10
- Romans 8:18
- Philippians 1:6
- 2 Corinthians 4:17
- Romans 8:37

- Psalm 30:5

Final Declaration

- I may have been stripped, but I was never forgotten.
- I may have been emptied, but I was never erased.
- I may have walked through fire, but I did not burn.
- I am not what was lost—I am what is being rebuilt.
- I carry power. I carry purpose. I carry prophetic proof that God restores.
- I am not defeated.
- I am rising.
- I am sent.
- My best is still ahead.

www.ingramcontent.com/pod-product-compliance
Lightning Source LLC
LaVergne TN
LVHW021500080426
835509LV00018B/2356
9781965635766